The Poems of Catullus

THE

POEMS

OF

CATULLUS:

SELECTED AND PREPARED

FOR THE USE OF SCHOOLS AND COLLEGES.

Fordyce Mitchell

BY F. M. HUBBARD,

Teacher of a Classical School, Boston.

BOSTON:

PUBLISHED BY PERKINS & MARVIN.

PHILADELPHIA: HENRY PERKINS.

1836.

Entered according to Act of Congress, in the year 1836,
By PERKINS & MARVIN,
in the Clerk's Office of the District Court of Massachusetts.

PREFACE.

THE text of this edition of Catullus is that
of Doering as reprinted in the Regent's Classics; which though not in all respects the
most perfect, is thought on the whole best
suited to students in this country. In a few
passages, a different and better reading has
been introduced, principally from Isaac Voss
and Sillig. The most important of these
changes are referred to in the notes.

By far the greater part of the poems of
Catullus are given in this edition. In making
a selection from them, the editor has been
desirous to retain every thing which could
exhibit his author in his personal character
and poetical powers, or throw light upon the

tures and sentiments of his age, and at the
same time to exclude all that might offend
by its indelicacy, or corrupt by its licentiousness.

Most of their poetry was written by the
ancients with so clear a perception of the
true principles of art and so skilful an application of them, that very seldom can a
part be taken away, without destroying the
unity and essentially impairing the beauty of
the whole. This is particularly true of their
epigrams, lyrics, and all sportive effusions of
fancy or feeling. The editor, therefore,
while he has made his selections numerous
and various enough to show all the peculiar
powers, and retain the finest productions of
Catullus, has deemed it but justice to him, as
well as required by good taste and just criticism, to present no fragments of poems. In
compliance with this sentiment, he has omitted entirely some poems, tainted in parts,
which as specimens of poetical skill it were
desirable to retain. This rule has been
scrupulously observed, except in one or two

instances, in which it was thought the canon would not strictly apply.

To each poem is prefixed a brief statement of the occasion of it, or an analysis of the scheme of thought it contains, which will be sufficient in general to guide the student to the true interpretation ; and as few students probably will read Catullus who have not made some attainments in classical antiquities, &c., many explanations have been omitted, which would be necessary for younger pupils. In selecting the passages to be illustrated, as well as the material and manner of illustration, the editor has been continually guided by the experience of intelligent pupils with whom he has read this author in his own school.

Boston, March, 1836.

METRES OF CATULLUS,

The different species of verse employed by Catullus, are thirteen.

I. The hexameter, consisting of six feet, of which the first four are either spondees or dactyles, the fifth a dactyle and the sixth a spondee. In Catullus the fifth is not unfrequently a spondee. The following scheme presents the construction.

$$- \cup \cup \quad - \cup \cup \quad - \cup \cup \quad - \cup \cup \quad - \cup \cup \quad - \cup$$
$$- - \qquad - - \qquad - - \qquad - - \qquad - - \qquad - \underset{\smile}{}$$

This is used alone, in Carm. 40 and 42.

II. The Pentameter, consisting of five feet, of which the first two are dactyles or spondees, the third a spondee, the last two anapaests. It is sometimes divided into *hemistichia*, or half verses, the first half consisting of two feet either dactyles

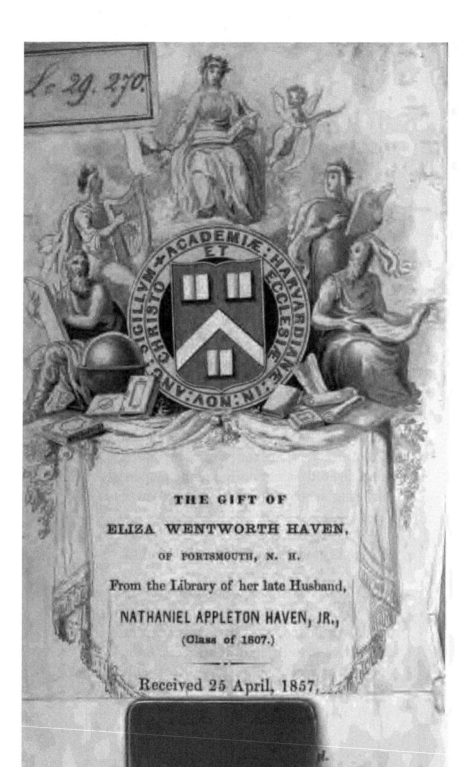

SIGILLVM · ACADEMIÆ · HARVARDIANÆ · IN · NOV · ANG · CHRISTO · ET · ECCLESIÆ

THE GIFT OF

ELIZA WENTWORTH HAVEN,

OF PORTSMOUTH, N. H.

From the Library of her late Husband,

NATHANIEL APPLETON HAVEN, JR.,

(Class of 1807.)

Received 25 April, 1857.

THE

POEMS

OF

CATULLUS:

SELECTED AND PREPARED

FOR THE USE OF SCHOOLS AND COLLEGES.

Fordyce Mitchell

BY F. M. HUBBARD,

Teacher of a Classical School, Boston.

BOSTON:

PUBLISHED BY PERKINS & MARVIN.
PHILADELPHIA: HENRY PERKINS.

1836.

PREFACE.

—◆—

THE text of this edition of Catullus is that
of Doering as reprinted in the Regent's Classics; which though not in all respects the
most perfect, is thought on the whole best
suited to students in this country. In a few
passages, a different and better reading has
been introduced, principally from Isaac Voss
and Sillig. The most important of these
changes are referred to in the notes.

By far the greater part of the poems of
Catullus are given in this edition. In making
a selection from them, the editor has been
desirous to retain every thing which could
exhibit his author in his personal character
and poetical powers, or throw light upon the

tastes and sentiments of his age, and at the same time to exclude all that might offend by its indelicacy, or corrupt by its licentiousness.

Most of their poetry was written by the ancients with so clear a perception of the true principles of art and so skilful an application of them, that very seldom can a part be taken away, without destroying the unity and essentially impairing the beauty of the whole. This is particularly true of their epigrams, lyrics, and all sportive effusions of fancy or feeling. The editor, therefore, while he has made his selections numerous and various enough to show all the peculiar powers, and retain the finest productions of Catullus, has deemed it but justice to him, as well as required by good taste and just criticism, to present no fragments of poems. In compliance with this sentiment, he has omitted entirely some poems, tainted in parts, which as specimens of poetical skill it were desirable to retain. This rule has been scrupulously observed, except in one or two

instances, in which it was thought the canon would not strictly apply.

To each poem is prefixed a brief statement of the occasion of it, or an analysis of the scheme of thought it contains, which will be sufficient in general to guide the student to the true interpretation; and as few students probably will read Catullus who have not made some attainments in classical antiquities, &c., many explanations have been omitted, which would be necessary for younger pupils. In selecting the passages to be illustrated, as well as the material and manner of illustration, the editor has been continually guided by the experience of intelligent pupils with whom he has read this author in his own school.

BOSTON, MARCH, 1836.

METRES OF CATULLUS,

ADAPTED AND ALTERED FROM VULPIUS' DIATRIBE DE METRIS CATULLI.

———

The different species of verse employed by Catullus, are thirteen.

I. The hexameter, consisting of six feet, of which the first four are either spondees or dactyles, the fifth a dactyle and the sixth a spondee. In Catullus the fifth is not unfrequently a spondee. The following scheme presents the construction.

$$-\cup\cup \quad -\cup\cup \quad -\cup\cup \quad -\cup\cup \quad -\cup\cup \quad -\cup$$
$$-- \quad\quad -- \quad\quad -- \quad\quad -- \quad\quad -- \quad\quad -\cup$$

This is used alone, in Carm. 40 and 42.

II. The Pentameter, consisting of five feet, of which the first two are dactyles or spondees, the third a spondee, the last two anapaests. It is sometimes divided into *hemistichia*, or half verses, the first half consisting of two feet either dactyles

THE

POEMS

OF

CATULLUS:

SELECTED AND PREPARED

FOR THE USE OF SCHOOLS AND COLLEGES.

Fordyce Mitchell

BY F. M. HUBBARD,

Teacher of a Classical School, Boston.

BOSTON:

PUBLISHED BY PERKINS & MARVIN.
PHILADELPHIA: HENRY PERKINS.

1836.

PREFACE.

The text of this edition of Catullus is that of Doering as reprinted in the Regent's Classics; which though not in all respects the most perfect, is thought on the whole best suited to students in this country. In a few passages, a different and better reading has been introduced, principally from Isaac Voss and Sillig. The most important of these changes are referred to in the notes.

By far the greater part of the poems of Catullus are given in this edition. In making a selection from them, the editor has been desirous to retain every thing which could exhibit his author in his personal character and poetical powers, or throw light upon the tastes and sentiments of his age, and at the same time to exclude all that might offend by its indelicacy, or corrupt by its licentiousness.

Most of their poetry was written by the ancients with so clear a perception of the true principles of art and so skilful an application of them, that very seldom can a part be taken away, without destroying the unity and essentially impairing the beauty of the whole. This is particularly true of their epigrams, lyrics, and all sportive effusions of fancy or feeling. The editor, therefore, while he has made his selections numerous and various enough to show all the peculiar powers, and retain the finest productions of Catullus, has deemed it but justice to him, as well as required by good taste and just criticism, to present no fragments of poems. In compliance with this sentiment, he has omitted entirely some poems, tainted in parts, which as specimens of poetical skill it were desirable to retain. This rule has been scrupulously observed, except in one or two

instances, in which it was thought the canon would not strictly apply.

To each poem is prefixed a brief statement of the occasion of it, or an analysis of the scheme of thought it contains, which will be sufficient in general to guide the student to the true interpretation ; and as few students probably will read Catullus who have not made some attainments in classical antiquities, &c., many explanations have been omitted, which would be necessary for younger pupils. In selecting the passages to be illustrated, as well as the material and manner of illustration, the editor has been continually guided by the experience of intelligent pupils with whom he has read this author in his own school.

BOSTON, MARCH, 1836.

METRES OF CATULLUS,

ADAPTED AND ALTERED FROM VULPIUS' DIATRIBE
DE METRIS CATULLI.

———————

The different species of verse employed by Catullus, are thirteen.

I. The hexameter, consisting of six feet, of which the first four are either spondees or dactyles, the fifth a dactyle and the sixth a spondee. In Catullus the fifth is not unfrequently a spondee. The following scheme presents the construction.

$$-\cup\cup \quad -\cup\cup \quad -\cup\cup \quad -\cup\cup \quad -\cup\cup \quad -\cup$$
$$-- \quad -- \quad -- \quad -- \quad -- \quad -\underset{\smile}{}$$

This is used alone, in Carm. 40 and 42.

II. The Pentameter, consisting of five feet, of which the first two are dactyles or spondees, the third a spondee, the last two anapæests. It is sometimes divided into *hemistichia*, or half verses, the first half consisting of two feet either dactyles

or spondees and a long syllable, the last of two
dactyles and a long or short syllable. We give a
scheme of both varieties.

I. $-\cup\cup$ $-\cup\cup$ $--$ $\cup\cup-$ $\cup\cup\underline{\cup}$
    $--$ $--$ $--$

II. $-\cup\cup$ $-\cup\cup$ $-$ $-\cup\cup$ $-\cup\cup$ $\underline{\cup}$
    $--$ · $--$

The Pentameter is employed in alternate verses
with the hexameters, in Carmen 43, and all the
other poems to the end. Some of the pentameters
of Catullus are quite harsh. The cæsura is often
neglected.

III. The Phalæcian commonly called the Phalæcian hendecasyllable, consisting of five feet, a
spondee, dactyle and three trochees. In the first
foot a trochee or an iambus is sometimes admitted,
and in the second, but rarely, a spondee.

$--$ $-\cup\cup$ $-\cup$ $-\cup$ $-\underline{\cup}$
$-\cup$ $--$
$\cup-$ ·

Catullus has used this verse more frequently
than any other in Carm. 1, 2, 3, 5, 6, 7, 8, 9, 10,
11, 17, 18, 20, 21, 25, 26, 27, 30, 31, 32, 33, 34. A
species called pseudo Phalæcian, occurs with the
pure Phalæcian in Carm. 37. It differs from the
pure in that the first foot may be a tribrachys, and
the second a trochee, and often a spondee.

IV. The Iambic Trimeter. It has six feet, properly each an Iambus. It admits however in the first, third, and fifth places a spondee, or its solutions the dactyle and anapaest. These varieties are not all used by Catullus. Carmen 4, 15, are pure Iambics. Carmen 36, is mixed with spondees. This measure is used in these three only.

⏑— ⏑— ⏑— ⏑— ⏑— ⏑—
‒— ‒— ‒—

V. Scazon, or Choliambus (χωλίαμβος i. e. lame iambus,) which coincides with the Iambic Trimeter, except that the fifth foot is always an iambus, and the sixth a spondee, or seldom a trochee.

⏑— ⏑— ⏑— ⏑— ⏑— —⏒
‒— ‒—

This measure is found in Carm. 16, 23, 28, 29.

VI. The Iambic Tetrameter catalectic, consisting of seven feet, which may be varied as in the Iambic Trimeter, and an additional syllable. Carmen 19 is in this measure. (The third line has an amphibrachys in the second place.)

VII. The Sapphic has five feet, a trochee, spondee, dactyle, trochee, and trochee or spondee. The second foot is sometimes a trochee.

—⏑ —— —⏑⏑ —⏑ —⏒
—⏑

VIII. The Adonic, properly a dactylic dimeter catalectic which is formed of a dactyle and a spondee.

$$- \cup \cup \ - \ \underline{\cup}$$

This is never used by itself, but in combination with the Sapphic forms what is called the Sapphic stanza. We find it in Carmen 35.

IX. The choriambic pentameter,* which consists of a spondee, three choriambi, and a pyrrich or iambus.

$$- - \ \ - \cup \cup - \ \ - \cup \cup - \ \ - \cup \cup - \ \ \cup \cup$$
$$\cup -$$

Carmen 22, is in this measure.

X. The Glyconic or choriambic trimeter, which consists of three feet, a spondee, choriambus, and iambus. The first foot is often a trochee, and sometimes an iambus.

$$- - \ \ - \cup \cup - \ \ \cup -$$
$$\cup -.$$
$$- \cup$$

It is used with other measures in Carm. 24, and 39.

XI. The Pherecratian, which consists of three feet, a spondee, dactyle and spondee. In Catullus

---

* So called by Carey, and by Scheller, *Alcaicus*.

the first foot is often a trochee, and sometimes an iambus, and the second in one verse a spondee.

$$-\,-\quad-\,\cup\,\cup\quad-\,-$$
$$-\,\cup$$
$$\cup\,-$$

It may be divided as a choriambic monometer hypercatalectic, with a basis usually a spondee.

$$-\,-\quad-\,\cup\,\cup\,-\quad-$$

This is combined with the Glyconic in Carm. 24, 39.

XII. The Priapean. It has six feet, a trochee, dactyle, amphimacer, trochee, dactyle, trochee. The first foot is sometimes a spondee, the third a dactyle, and the fourth a spondee.

$$-\,\cup\;'\;-\,\cup\,\cup\quad-\,\cup\,-\quad-\,\cup\quad-\,\cup\,\cup\quad-\,\cup$$
$$-\,-\qquad\qquad-\,\cup\,\cup\quad-\,-$$

Used in Carm. 12, 13, 14.

XIII. The Galliambic, a loose kind of measure, which is used by no Latin poet except Catullus, and by him only in Carmen 41. It derives its name from the *Galli* priests of Cybele. It consists of six feet, of which the first is usually an anapaest, sometimes a spondee or tribrachys, the second an iambus, rarely an anapaest, tribrachys, or dactyle, the third an iambus or spondee, the fourth a dactyle or spondee, the fifth a dactyle or

amphimacer or spondee, the sixth an anapaest, or
an iambus preceded by an amphimacer.

Carey divides it into two iambic dimeters catalectic, the first beginning with a spondee or an
anapàest, and ending with a long syllable, the
second wanting the last syllable; and gives this
scheme.

$$- \cup - \quad \cup - \quad - \quad - \cup - \quad \cup -$$
$$\cup \cup - \quad \cup \cup \cup \qquad \cup \cup - \quad \cup \cup \cup$$
$$\cup \cup \cup$$

sŭpĕr ăl | tă vēc | tŭs ā | tȳs || cĕlĕrī | rătĕ mă | rĭa

Catullus makes very frequent use of elisions,
ecthlipses and other figures of scanning.

C. VALERII CATULLI

VERONENSIS

CARMINA.

CARMEN I.

Ad Cornelium Nepotem.

Quoi dono lepidum novum libellum,
Aridâ modo pumice expolitum?
Corneli, tibi: namque tu solebas
Meas esse aliquid putare nugas,
Jam tum, cum ausus es, unus Italorum,   5
Omne ævum tribus explicare chartis,
Doctis, Jupiter! et laboriosis.
Quare habe tibi, quidquid hoc libelli est,
Qualecumque; quod, o patrona Virgo,
Plus uno maneat perenne sæclo.   10

CARMEN II.

Ad Passerem Lesbiæ.

Passer, deliciæ meæ puellæ,
Quîcum ludere, quem in sinu tenere,
Quoi primum digitum dare appetenti,
Et acres solet incîtare morsus;
Cum desiderio meo nitenti   5
Carum nescio-quid lubet jocari,
Et solatiolum sui doloris
Credo, ut tum gravis acquiescat ardor.
Tecum ludere, sicut ipsa, posse,
Et tristes animi levare curas,   10
Tam gratum mihi, quam ferunt puellæ
Pernici aureolum fuisse malum,
Quod zonam soluït diu ligatam.

CARMEN III.

Luctus in Morte Passeris.

Lugete, o Veneres, Cupidinesque,
Et quantum est hominum venustiorum!
Passer mortuus est meæ puellæ,
Passer, deliciæ meæ puellæ,

Quem plus illa oculis suis amabat :   5
Nam mellitus erat, suamque nôrat
Ipsam tam bene, quam puella matrem :
Nec sese a gremio illius movebat ;
Sed circumsiliens modo huc, modo illuc,
Ad solam dominam usque pipilabat.   10
Qui nunc it, per iter tenebricosum,
Illuc, unde negant redire quemquam.
At vobis male sit, malæ tenebræ ·
Orci, quæ omnia bella devoratis !
Tam bellum mihi passerem abstulistis !   15
O factum male ! O miselle passer !
Tuâ nunc operâ meæ puellæ
Flendo turgiduli rubent ocelli.

CARMEN IV.

Dedicatio Phaseli.

Phaselus ille, quem videtis, hospites,
Ait fuisse navium celerrimus, ·
Neque ullius natantis impetum trabis
Nequîsse præterire, sive palmulis
Opus foret volare, sive linteo.   5
Et hoc negat minacis Adriatici
Negare litus, insulasve Cycladas,

Rhodumve nobilem, horridamve Thraciam,
Propontida, trucemve Ponticum sinum;
Ubi iste, post phaselus, antea fuit   10
Comata silva : nam, Cytorio in jugo,
Loquente sæpe sibilum edidit comâ.
Amastri Pontica, et Cytore buxifer,
Tibi hæc fuisse et esse cognitissima
Ait phaselus : ultimâ ex origine   15
Tuô stetisse dicit in cacumine,
Tuo imbuisse palmulas in æquore,
Et inde tot per impotentia freta
Herum tulisse; læva, sive dextera
Vocaret aura, sive utrumque Jupiter   20
Simul secundus incidisset in pedem;
Neque ulla vota litoralibus Diis
Sibi esse facta, cum veniret a mare
Novissimo hunc ad usque limpidum lacum.
Sed hæc prius fuêre : nunc recondita   25
Senet quiete, seque dedicat tibi,
Gemelle Castor, et gemelle Castoris.

CARMEN V.

Ad Lesbiam.

Vivamus, mea Lesbia, atque amemus;
Rumoresque senum severiorum

Omnes unius æstimemus assis.
Soles occidere et redire possunt :
Nobis, cum semel occidit brevis lux,   5
Nox est perpetua una dormienda.
Da mî basia mille, deinde centum :
Dein mille altera, dein secunda centum,
Dein usque altera mille, deinde centum :
Dein, cum millia multa fecerimus,   10
Conturbabimus illa, ne sciamus,
Aut ne quis malus invidere possit,
Cum tantum sciat esse basiorum.

CARMEN VI.

Ad Lesbiam.

Quæris, quot mihi basiationes
Tuæ, Lesbia, sint satis superque?
Quam magnus numerus Libyssæ arenæ
Laserpiciferis jacet Cyrenis,
Oraclum Jovis inter æstuosi   5
Et Batti veteris sacrum sepulcrum ;
Aut quam sidera multa, cum tacet nox,
Furtivos hominum vident amores ;
Tam te basia multa basiare,
Vesano satis et super Catullo est,   10

1 *

Quæ nec pernumerare curiosi
Possint, nec mala fascinare lingua.

CARMEN VII.

Ad Verannium.

Veranni, omnibus e meis amicis
Antistans mihi millibus trecentis,
Venistine domum ad tuos Penates,
Fratresque unanimos, anumque matrem ?
Venisti.   O mihi nuntii beati !   5
Visam te incolumem ; audiamque Iberûm
Narrantem loca, facta, nationes,
Ut mos est tuus ; applicansque collum,
Jucundum os oculosque suaviabor.
O, quantum est hominum beatiorum !   10
Quid me lætius est, beatiusve ?

CARMEN VIII.

De Varri Scorto.

Varrus me meus ad suos amores
Visum duxerat e foro otiosum ;
Scortillum (ut mihi tum repente visum est)

Non sane illepidum, nec invenustum.
Huc ut venimus, incidêre nobis   5
Sermones varii; in quibus, quid esset
Jam Bithynia, quomodo se haberet,
Et quonam mihi profuisset ære?
Respondi (id, quod erat) nihil neque ipsis
Nec prætoribus esse, nec cohorti,   10
Cur quisquam caput unctius referret;
Præsertim quibus esset irrumator
Prætor, nec faceret pili cohortem. ·
At certe tamen, inquiunt, quod illic
Natum dicitur esse, comparâsti   15
Ad lecticam homines.   Ego, ut puellæ
Unum me facerem beatiorem,
Non, inquam, mihi tam fuit maligne,
Ut, provincia quod mala incidisset,
Non possem octo homines parare rectos.   20
At mî nullus erat neque hîc neque illic,
Fractum qui veteris pedem grabati
In collo sibi collocare posset.
Hîc illa, ut decuit cinædiorem,
Quæso, inquit, mihi, mi Catulle, paulum   25
Istos commoda; nam volo ad Serapin
Deferri.   Mane, inquii puellæ:
Istud, quod modo dixeram me habere,
Fugit me ratio: meus sodalis

Cinna est Caïus : is sibi paravit. 30
Verum, utrum illius an mei, quid ad me?
Utor tam bene, quam mihi parârim.
Sed tu insulsa male et molesta vivis,
Per quam non licet esse negligentem.

CARMEN IX.

Ad Asinium.

Marrucine Asini, manu sinistrâ
Non belle uteris in joco atque vino :
Tollis lintea negligentiorum.
Hoc salsum esse putas? Fugit te, inepte ;
Quamvis sordida res et invenusta est. 5
Non credis mihi? Crede Pollioni
Fratri, qui tua furta vel talento
Mutari velit : est enim leporum
Disertus puer, ac facetiarum.
Quare aut hendecasyllabos trecentos 10
Exspecta, aut mihi linteum remitte ;
Quod me non movet æstimatione,
Verum est mnemosynon mei sodalis :
Nam sudaria Setaba ex Iberis
Miserunt mihi muneri Fabullus 15
Et Verannius. Hæc amem necesse est,
Ut Veranniolum meum et Fabullum.

CARMEN X.

Ad Fabullum.

Cœnabis bene, mi Fabulle, apud me · .
Paucis, si tibi Dî favent, diebus,
Si tecum attuleris bonam atque magnam
Cœnam, non sine candidâ puellâ,
Et vino et sale, et omnibus cachinnis.   5
Hæc si, inquam, attuleris, venuste noster,
Cœnabis bene ; nam tui Catulli   .
Plenus sacculus est aranearum.
Sed contra accipies meros amores,
Seu quid suavius elegantiusve est ;   10
Nam unguentum dabo, quod meæ puellæ
Donârunt Veneres Cupidinesque ;
Quod tu cum olfacies, Deos rogabis,
Totum ut te faciant, Fabulle, nasum.

CARMEN XI.

Ad Calvum Licinium.

Ni te plus oculis meis amarem,
Jucundissime Calve, munere isto
Odissem te odio Vatiniano.

Nam quid feci ego, quidve sum locutus,
Cur me tot male perderes poëtis?   5
Isti Dî mala multa dent clienti,
Qui tantum tibi misit impiorum.
Quod si (ut suspicor) hoc novum ac repertum
Munus dat tibi Sulla literator,
Non est mî male, sed bene ac beate,   10
Quod non dispereunt tui labores.
Dî magni! horribilem et sacrum libellum!
Quem tu scilicet ad tuum Catullum
Mîsti, continuo ut die periret,
Saturnalibus, optimo dierum.   15
Non, non hoc tibi, salse, sic abibit:
Nam, si luxerit, ad librariorum
Curram scrinia; Cæsios, Aquinios,
Suffenum, omnia colligam venena,
Ac te his suppliciis remunerabor.   20
Vos hinc interea valete, abite
Illuc, unde malum pedem tulistis,
Sæcli incommoda, pessimi poëtæ!

CARMEN XII.

Ad Coloniam.

O Colonia, quæ cupis ponte ludere longo,
Et salire paratum habes; sed vereris inepta

Crura ponticuli asculis stantis, irredivivus
Ne supinus eat, cavâque in palude recumbat;
Sic tibi bonus ex tuâ pons libidine fiat,   5
In quo vel Salisubsulis sacra suscipiantur:
Munus hoc mihi maximi da, Colonia, risûs.
Quemdam municipem meum de tuo volo ponte
Ire præcipitem in lutum, per caputque pedesque;
Verum totius ut lacûs, putidæque paludis,   10
Lividissima, maximeque est profunda vorago.
Insulsissimus est homo; nec sapit pueri instar
Bimuli, tremulâ patris dormientis in ulnâ.
Quoi cum sit viridissimo nupta flore puella,
Et puella tenellulo delicatior hædo,   15
Asservanda nigerrimis diligentius uvis;
Ludere hanc sinit, ut lubet, nec pili facit uni;
Nec se sublevat ex suâ parte: sed, velut alnus
In fossâ Ligurî jacet suppernata securi,
Tantumdem omnia sentiens, quam si nulla sit
     usquam;   20
Talis iste meus stupor nil videt, nihil audit.
Ipse qui sit, utrum sit, an non sit, id quoque nescit.
Nunc eum volo de tuo ponte mittere pronum,
Si pote stolidum repente excitare veternum,
Et supinum animum in gravi derelinquere
     cœno,   25
Ferream ut soleam tenaci in voragine mula.

CARMEN XIII.

Ad Hortorum Deum.

Hunc lucum tibi dedico, consecroque, Priape,
Quâ domus tua Lampsaci est, quâque silva,
 Priape.
Nam te præcipue in suis urbibus colit ora
Hellespontia, cæteris ostreosior oris.

CARMEN XIV.

Hortorum Deus.

Hunc ego, juvenes, locum, villulamque palustrem,
Tectam vimine junceo, caricisque maniplis,
Quercus arida, rusticâ conformata securi,
Nutrivi, magis et magis ut beata quotannis.
Hujus nam domini colunt me, Deumque salu-
 tant,   5
Pauperis tugurî pater, filiusque * * *
Alter assiduâ colens diligentiâ, ut herba
Dumosa asperaque a meo sit remota sacello ;
Alter parva ferens manu semper munera largâ.
Florido mihi ponitur picta vere corolla   10
Primitu', et tenerâ virens spica mollis aristâ :

Luteæ violæ mihi, luteumque papaver,
Pallentesque cucurbitæ, et suave olentia mala;
Uva pampineâ rubens educata sub umbrâ:
Sanguine hanc etiam mihi (sed tacebitis) aram 15
Barbatus linit hirculus, cornipesque capella;
Pro quîs omnia honoribus hæc necesse Priapo
Præstare, et domini hortulum, vineamque tueri.
Quare hinc, o pueri, malas abstinete rapinas.
Vicinus prope dives est, negligensque Priapus. 20
Inde sumite: semita hæc deinde vos feret ipsa.

CARMEN XV.

Hortorum Deus.

Ego hæc, ego arte fabricata rusticâ,
Ego arida, o viator, ecce populus
Agellulum hunc, sinistra, tute quem vides,
Herique villulam, hortulumque pauperis
Tuor, malasque furis arceo manus.   5
Mihi corolla picta vere ponitur,
Mihi rubens arista sole fervido,
Mihi virente dulcis uva pampino,
Mihique glauca duro oliva frigore.
Meis capella delicata pascuis   10
In urbem adulta lacte portat ubera;

2

Meisque pinguis agnus ex ovilibus
Gravem domum remittit ære dexteram ;
Teneraque, matre mugiente, vaccula
Deûm profundit ante templa sanguinem. 15
Proin', viator, hunc Deum vereberis,
Manumque sorsum habebis.

CARMEN XVI.

Ad Varrum.

Suffenus iste, Varre, quem probe nôsti,
Homo est venustus, et dicax, et urbanus ;
Idemque longe plurimos facit versus.
Puto esse ego illi millia aut decem aut plura
Perscripta ; nec sic, ut fit, in palimpsesto 5
Relata : chartæ regiæ, novi libri,
Novi umbilici, lora rubra, membrana
Directa plumbo, et pumice omnia æquata.
Hæc cum legas, tum bellus ille et urbanus
Suffenus, unus caprimulgus aut fossor 10
Rursus videtur : tantum abhorret, ac mutat.
Hoc quid putemus esse ? qui modo scurra,
Aut siquid hac re tritius, videbatur,
Idem inficeto est inficetior rure,
Simul poëmata attigit : neque idem unquam 15
Æque est beatus, ac poëma cum scribit :

Tam gaudet in se, tamque se ipse miratur.
Nimirum idem omnes fallimur ; neque est quis-
    quam,
Quem non in aliquâ re videre Suffenum
Possis.   Suus quoique attributus est error :   20
Sed non videmus, manticæ quod in tergo est.

CARMEN XVII.

Ad Furium.

Furi, quoi neque servus est, neque arca,
Nec cimex, neque araneus, neque ignis ;
Verum est et pater; et noverca, quorum
Dentes vel silicem comesse possunt ;
Est pulchre tibi cum tuo parente,   5
Et cum conjuge ligneâ parentis.
Nec mirum : bene nam valetis omnes :
Pulchre concoquitis ; nihil timetis ;
Non incendia, non graves ruinas,
Non facta impia, non dolos veneni,   10
Non casus alios periculorum.
Atqui corpora sicciora cornu,
Aut, siquid magis aridum est, habetis,
Sole, et frigore, et esuritione.
Quare non tibi sit bene ac beate ?   15
A te sudor abest, abest saliva,

Mucusque, et mala pituita nasi.
Hæc tu commoda tam beata, Furi,
Noli spernere, nec putare parvi ;
Et sestertia, quæ soles, precari   20
Centum desine ; nam sat es beatus.

CARMEN XVIII.

Ad Juventium Puerum.

O qui flosculus es Juventiorum,
Non horum modo, sed quot aut fuerunt,
Aut posthac aliis erunt in annis !
Mallem divitias mihi dedisses
Isti, quoi neque servus est neque arca,   5
Quam sic te sineres ab illo amari.
Quî ? non est homo bellus ? inquies.　Est :
Sed bello huic neque servus est neque arca.
Hæc tu, quam lubet, abjice, elevaque ;
Nec servum tamen ille habet neque arcam. 10

CARMEN XIX.

Ad Thallum.

Cinæde Thalle, mollior cuniculi capillo,
Vel anseris medullulâ, vel imulâ oricillâ,

Idemque, Thalle, turbidâ rapacior procellâ,
Cum diva mulier aves ostendit occinentes !
Remitte pallium mihi, meum quod involâsti, 5
Sudariumque Setabum, catagraphosque Thynos,
Inepte, quæ palam soles habere, tanquam avita ;
Quæ nunc tuis ab unguibus reglutina, et remitte,
Ne laneum latusculum, manusque mollicellas,
Inusta turpiter tibi flagella conscribillent, 10
Et insolenter æstues, velut minuta magno
Deprensa navis in mari, vesaniente vento.

CARMEN XX.

Ad Furium.

Furi, villula [nostra] non ad Austri
Flatus opposita est, nec ad Favonî,
Nec sævi Boreæ, aut Apeliotæ,
Verum ad millia quindecim et ducentos.
O ventum horribilem atque pestilentem ! 5

CARMEN XXI.

Ad Pocillatorem Puerum.

Minister vetuli, puer, Falerni,
Inger' mî calices amariores,

2 *

Ut lex Postumiæ jubet magistræ,
Ebriosâ acinâ ebriosioris.
At vos, quo lubet, hinc abite, lymphæ,   5
Vini pernicies, et ad severos
Migrate : hic merus est Thyonianus.

CARMEN XXII.

Ad Alphenum.

Alphene immemor, atque unanimis false sodal-
          ibus !
Jam te nil miseret, dure, tui dulcis amiculi :
Jam me prodere, jam non dubitas fallere, perfide!
Nec facta impia fallacûm hominum Cœlicolis
          placent ;
Quæ tu negligis, ac me miserum deseris in
          malis.   5
Eheu ! quid faciant dehinc homines, quoive hab-
          eant fidem ?
Certe tute jubebas animam tradere, inique, me
Inducens in amorem, quasi tuta omnia mî forent.
Idem nunc retrahis te ; ac tua dicta omnia fac-
          taque
Ventos irrita ferre, et nebulas aërias, sinis.   10
Si tu oblitus es, at Dî meminerunt, meminit
          Fides,
Quæ, te ut pœniteat postmodo facti, faciet, tui.

CARMEN XXIII.

Ad Sirmionem Pœninsulam.

Pæninsularum, Sirmio, insularumque
Ocelle, quascumque in liquentibus stagnis,
Marique vasto, fert uterque Neptunus!
Quam te libenter, quamque lætus, inviso!
Vix mî ipse credens, Thyniam atque Bithynos 5
Liquisse campos, et videre te in tuto,
O! quid solutis est beatius curis?
Cum mens onus reponit, ac peregrino
Labore fessi venimus larem ad nostrum,
Desideratoque acquiescimus lecto.   10
Hoc est, quod unum est pro laboribus tantis.
Salve, o venusta Sirmio! atque hero gaude:
Gaudete vosque, Lydiæ lacus undæ:
Ridete, quidquid est domi cachinnorum.

CARMEN XXIV.

Ad Dianam.

Dianæ sumus in fide
Puellæ, et pueri integri:
Dianam pueri integri,
    Puellæque, canamus.

O Latonia, maximi   5
Magna progenies Jovis!
Quam mater prope Deliam
    Deposivit olivam;
Montium domina ut fores,
Silvarumque virentium,   10
Saltuumque reconditorum,
    Amniumque sonantûm.
Tu Lucina dolentibus
Juno dicta puerperis:
Tu potens Trivia, et notho es   15
    Dicta lumine Luna.
Tu, cursu, Dea, menstruo
Metiens iter annuum,
Rustica agricolæ bonis
    Tecta frugibus exples.   20
Sis quocumque placet tibi
Sancta nomine; Romulique
Antiquam, ut solita es, bonâ
    Sospites ope gentem.

CARMEN XXV.

Cæcilium invitat.

Poëtæ tenero, meo sodali,
Velim Cæcilio, papyre, dicas,

Veronam veniat; Novi relinquens
Comi mœnia, Lariumque litus :
Nam quasdam volo cogitationes 5
Amici accipiat sui, meique.
Quare, si sapiet, viam vorabit,
Quamvis candida millies puella
Euntem revocet, manusque collo
Ambas injiciens, roget morari; 10
Quæ nunc (si mihi vera nuntiantur)
Illum deperit impotente amore.
Nam, quo tempore legit inchoatam
Dindymi dominam, ex eo misellæ
Ignes interiorem edunt medullam. 15
Ignosco tibi, Sapphicâ puella
Musâ doctior ; est enim venuste
Magna Cæcilio inchoata Mater.

CARMEN XXVI.

In Annales Volusii.

Annales Volusî,
Votum solvite pro meâ puellâ :
Nam sanctæ Veneri Cupidinique
Vovit, si sibi restitutus essem,

Desîssemque truces vibrare iambos,　　　5
Electissima pessimi poëtæ
Scripta tardipedi Deo daturam
Infelicibus ustulanda lignis :
Et hæc pessima se puella vidit
Jocose et lepide vovere Divis.　　　10
Nunc, o cœruleo creata ponto !
Quæ sanctum Idalium, Syrosque apertos,
Quæque Ancona, Cnidumque arundinosam
Colis, quæque Amathunta, quæque Golgos,
Quæque Dyrrhachium Adriæ tabernam ;　15
Acceptum face, redditumque votum,
Si non illepidum, neque invenustum est.
At vos interea venite in ignem,
Pleni ruris et inficetiarum,
Annales Volusî.　　　20

CARMEN XXVII.

Ad Cornificium.

Male est, Cornifici, tuo Catullo :
Male est, mehercule, et laboriose,
Et magis magis in dies et horas :
Quem tu, quod minimum facillimumque est,
Quâ solatus es allocutione ?　　　5

Irascor tibi. Sic meos amores . . . . . ?
Paulum quid lubet allocutionis,
Mœstius lacrymis Simonìdeis.

CARMEN XXVIII.

In Egnatium.

Egnatius, quod candidos habet dentes,
Renidet usquequâque. Seu ad rei ventum est
Subsellium, cum orator excitat fletum,
Renidet ille ; seu pii ad rogum filî
Lugetur, orba cum flet unicum mater,   5
Renidet ille : quidquid est, ubicumque est,
Quodcumque agit, renidet. Hunc habet morbum,
Neque elegantem, ut arbitror, neque urbanum.
Quare monendus es mihi, bone Egnati :
Si urbanus esses, aut Sabinus, aut Tiburs,   10
Aut pastus Umber, aut obesus Etruscus,
Aut Lanuvinus ater atque dentatus,
Aut Transpadanus, (ut meos quoque attingam)
Aut quilibet, qui puriter lavit dentes ;
Tamen renidere usquequâque te nollem :   15
Nam risu inepto res ineptior nulla est.

CARMEN XXIX.

Ad Fundum suum.

O funde noster, seu Sabine, seu Tiburs,
Nam te esse Tiburtem autumant, quibus non est
Cordi Catullum lædere ; at, quibus cordi est,
Quovis Sabinum pignore esse contendunt.
Sed, seu Sabine, sive verius Tiburs,   5
Fui libenter in tuâ suburbanâ
Villâ, malámque pectore expuli tussim ;
Non immerenti quam mihi meus venter,
Dum sumtuosas appeto, dedit, cœnas.
Nam, Sextianus dum volo esse conviva,   10
Orationem in Antium petitorem,
Plenam véneni et pestilentiæ, legit.
Hîc me gravedo frigida, et frequens tussis
Quassavit, usquedum in tuum sinum fugi,
Et me recuravi otioque et urticâ.   15
Quare refectus maximas tibi grates
Ago, meum quod non es ulta peccatum.
Nec deprecor jam, si nefaria scripta
Sextî recepso, quin gravediñem et tussim,
Non mî, sed ipsi Sextio, ferat frigus,   20
Qui tunc vocat me, cum malum legit librum.

CARMEN XXX.

Ad se ipsum, de Adventu Veris.

Jam ver egelidos refert tepores ;
Jam cœli furor æquinoctialis
Jucundis Zephyri silescit auris.
Linquantur Phrygii, Catulle, campi,
Nicææque ager uber æstuosæ.   5
Ad claras Asiæ volemus urbes.
Jam mens prætrepidans avet vagari ;
Jam læti studio pedes vigescunt.
O dulces comitum valete cœtus,
Longe quos simul a domo profectos   10
Diverse variæ viæ reportant.

CARMEN XXXI.

Ad Porcium et Socrationem.

Porci et Socration, duæ sinistræ
Pisonis, scabies famesque Memmî,
Vos Veranniolo meo et Fabullo
Verpus præposuit Priapus ille ?
Vos convivia lauta sumtuose   5
De die facitis ; mei sodales
Quærunt in triviis vocationes ?

3

CARMEN XXXII.

Ad Juventium.

Mellitos oculos tuos, Juventi,
Siquis me sinat usque basiare,
Usque ad millia basiem trecenta;
Nec unquam saturum inde cor futurum est;
Non, si densior aridis aristis   5
Sit nostræ seges osculationis.

CARMEN XXXIIL

Ad M. T. Ciceronem.

Disertissime Romuli nepotum,
Quot sunt, quotque fuêre, Marce Tulli,
Quotque post aliis erunt in annis;
Gratias tibi maximas Catullus
Agit, pessimus omnium poëta;   5
Tanto pessimus omnium poëta,
Quanto tu optimus omnium patronus.

CARMEN XXXIV.

Ad Licinium.

Hesterno, Licini, die otiosi
Multum lusimus in meis tabellis,

Ut convenerat esse ; delicatos
Scribens versiculos, uterque nostrûm
Ludebat numero modo hoc, modo illoc,   5
Reddens mutua per jocum atque vinum.
Atque illinc abii, tuo lepore
Incensus, Licini, facetiisque,
Ut nec me miserum cibus juvaret,
Nec somnus tegeret quiete ocellos ;   10
Sed toto indomitus furore lecto
Versarer, cupiens videre lucem,
Ut tecum loquerer, simulque ut essem.
At, defessa labore membra postquam
Semimortua lectulo jacebant,   15
Hoc, jucunde, tibi poëma feci,
Ex quo perspiceres meum dolorem.
Nunc audax, cave, sis ; precesque nostras,
Oramus, cave, despuas, ocelle,
Ne pœnas Nemesis reposcat a te :   20
Est vehemens Dea ; lædere hanc caveto.

CARMEN XXXV.
Ad Lesbiam.

Ille mî par esse Deo videtur,
Ille (si fas est) superare Divos,
Qui, sedens adversus, identidem te
    Spectat et audit

Dulce ridentem; misero quod omnes   5
Eripit sensus mihi: nam, simul te,
Lesbia, adspexi, nihil est super mî
     [* *Vocis in ore :* *]
Lingua sed torpet: tenuis sub artus
Flamma dimanat: sonitu suopte   10
Tintinant aures: geminâ teguntur
     Lumina nocte.
[*Otium, Catulle, tibi molestum est ;*
Otio exsultas, nimiumque gestis :
Otium et reges prius, et beatas   15
Perdidit urbes.]

CARMEN XXXVI.

Ad se ipsum, de Strumâ et Vatinio.

Quid est, Catulle, quid moraris emori?
Sellâ in curuli Struma Nonius sedet:
Per consulatum pejerat Vatinius.
Quid est, Catulle, quid moraris emori?

CARMEN XXXVII.

Ad Camerium.

Oramus, si forte non molestum est,
Demonstres ubi sint tuæ tenebræ.

Te quæsivimus in minore Campo,
Te in Circo, te in omnibus libellis,
Te in templo superi Jovis sacrato,   5
In Magni simul ambulatione :
Femellas omnes, amice, prendi,
Quas voltu vidi tamen sereno ;
Has [vel te sic] ipse flagitabam :
Camerium mihi, pessimæ puellæ.   10
Quædam inquit, nudum sinum reducens :
En hîc in roseis latet papillis.
Sed te jam ferre Herculei labos est :
Tanto te in fastu negas, amice.
Dic nobis, ubi sis futurus : ede,   15
Audacter committe, crede luci.
Num te lacteolæ tenent puellæ ?
Si linguam clauso tenes in ore,
Fructus projicies amoris omnes :
Verbosâ gaudet Venus loquelâ.   20
Vel, si vis, licet obseres palatum,
Dum vostri sim particeps amoris.
Non, custos si fingar ille Cretum,
Non si Pegaseo ferar volatu,
Non Ladas si ego, pennipesve Perseus,   25
Non Rhesi niveæ citæque bigæ ;
Adde huc plumipedes volatilesque,
Ventorumque simul require cursum,

     3 *

Quos junctos, Cameri, mihi dicares;
Defessus tamen omnibus medullis,   .   30
Et multis languoribus peresus
Essem, te, mi amice, quæritando.

CARMEN XXXVIII.

Num te leæna montibus Libyssinis,
Aut Scylla latrans infimâ inguinum parte,
Tam mente durâ procreavit ac tetrâ,
Ut supplicis vocem in novissimo casu
Contemtam haberes? O nimis fero corde!   5

CARMEN XXXIX.

In Nuptias Juliæ et Manlii.

Collis o Heliconei
Cultor, Uraniæ genus,
Qui rapis teneram ad virum
Virginem, o Hymenæe Hymen!
     Hymen o Hymenæe!   5
Cinge tempora floribus
Suaveolentis amaraci:
Flammeum cape: lætus huc,
Huc veni, niveo gerens
     Luteum pede soccum: 10

Excitusque hilari die,
Nuptialia concinens
Voce carmina tinnulâ,
Pelle humum pedibus; manu
    Pineam quate tædam.   15
Namque Julia Manlio
(Qualis Idalium colens
Venit ad Phrygium Venus
Judicem) bona cum bonâ
    Nubit alite virgo;   20
Floridis velut enitens
Myrtus Asia ramulis,
Quos Hamadryades Deæ
Ludicrum sibi roscido
    Nutriunt humore.   25
Quare age, huc aditum ferens,
Perge linquere Thespiæ
Rupis Aonios specus,
Lympha quos super irrigat
    Frigerans Aganippe: 30
Ac domum dominam voca,
Conjugis cupidam novi,
Mentem amore revinciens,
Ut tenax hedera huc et huc
    Arborem implicat errans.   35
Vos item simul, integræ

Virgines, quibus advenit
Par dies, agite, in modum
Dicite, O Hymenæe Hymen!
    Hymen o Hymenæe!   40
Ut lubentius, audiens
Se citarier ad suum
Munus, huc aditum ferat
Dux bonæ Veneris, boni
    Conjugator amoris.   45
Quis Deus magis, ah! magis
Est petendus amantibus?
Quem colent homines magis
Cœlitum? O Hymenæe Hymen!
    Hymen o Hymenæe!   50
Te suis tremulus parens
Invocat: tibi virgines
Zonulâ solüunt sinus:
Te, timens, cupidâ novus
    Captat aure maritus.   55
Tu fero juveni in manus
Floridam ipse puellulam
Matris e gremio suæ
Dedis, o Hymenæe Hymen!
    Hymen o Hymenæe!   60
Nil potest sine te Venus,
Fama quod bona comprobet,

Commodi capere : at potest,
Te volente.　Quis huic Deo
　　Compararier ausit ?　　　　　65
Nulla quit sine te domus
Liberos dare, nec parens
Stirpe jungier : at potest,
Te volente.　Quis huic Deo
　　Compararier ausit ?　　　　　70
Quæ tuis careat sacris,
Non queat dare præsides
Terra finibus : at queat,
Te volente.　Quis huic Deo
　　Compararier ausit ?　　　　　75
Claustra pandite januæ :
Virgo adest.　Vide'n', ut faces
Splendidas quatiunt comas ?
Sed moraris ; abit dies :
　　Prodeas, nova nupta.　　　　80
Tardat ingenuus pudor,
Quæ tamen magis audiens
Flet, quod ire necesse sit.
Sed moraris ; abit dies :
　　Prodeas, nova nupta.　　　　85
Flere desine.　Non tibi, Au-
runculeia, periculum est,
Nequa femina pulchrior

Clarum ab Oceano diem
    Viderit venientem.   90
Talis in vario solet
Divitis domini hortulo
Stare flos hyacinthinus.
Sed moraris; abit dies:
    Prodeas, nova nupta.   95
Prodeas, nova nupta, sis,
(Jam videtur) et audias
Nostra verba.   Vide'n'? faces
Aureas quatiunt comas.
    Prodeas, nova nupta.   100
Non tuus levis in malâ
Deditus vir adulterâ,
Probra turpia persequens,
A tuis teneris volet
    Secubare papillis;   105
Lenta, qui, velut assitas
Vitis implicat arbores,
Implicabitur in tuum
Complexum.   Sed abit dies:
    Prodeas, nova nupta.   110
       *   *   *
       *   *   *
       *   *   *
O cubile! quot [o nimis
    Candido pede lecti]   115

Quæ tuo veniunt hero,
Quanta gaudia, quæ vagâ
Nocte, quæ mediâ die
Gaudeat. Sed abit dies:
 Prodeas, nova nupta. 120
Tollite, o pueri, faces:
Flammeum video venire.
Ite, concinite in modum,
Io Hymen Hymenæe, io !
 Io Hymen Hymenæe ! 125
Neu diu taceat procax
Fescennina locutio ;
Neu nuces pueris neget,
Desertum domini audiens
 Concubinus amorem. 130
Da nuces pueris, iners
Concubine. Satis diu
Lusisti nucibus. Lubet
Jam servire Thalassio.
 Concubine, nuces da. 135
Sordebant tibi villuli,
Concubine, hodie atque heri:
Nunc tuum cinerarius
Tondet os. Miser, ah ! miser
 Concubine, nuces da. 140
Diceris male te a tuis,

Unguentate, glabris, marite
Abstinere : sed abstine.
Io Hymen Hymenæe, io !
  Io Hymen Hymenæe !   145
Scimus hæc tibi, quæ licent,
Sola cognita : sed marito
Ista non eadem licent.
Io Hymen Hymenæe, io !
  Io Hymen Hymenæe !   150
Nupta, tu quoque, quæ tuus
Vir petet, cave ne neges ;
Ne petitum aliunde eat.
Io Hymen Hymenæe, io !
  Io Hymen Hymenæe !   155
En tibi domus ut potens
Et beata viri tui,
Quæ tibi, sine, serviat,
(Io Hymen Hymenæe, io !
  Io Hymen Hymenæe !)   160
Usque dum tremulum movens
Cana tempus anilitas
Omnia omnibus annuit.
Io Hymen Hymenæ, io !
  Io Hymen Hymenæe !   165
Transfer, omine cum bono,
Limen aureolos pedes,

Rasilemque subi forem.
Io Hymen Hymenæe, io!
    Io Hymen Hymenæe !   170
Adspice, intus ut accubans
Vir tuus Tyrio in toro,
Totus immineat tibi.
Io Hymen Hymenæe, io!
    Io Hymen Hymenæe!   175
Illi, non minus ac tibi,
Pectore uritur intimo
Flamma, sed penite magis.
Io Hymen Hymenæe, io!
    Io Hymen Hymenæe!   180
Mitte brachiolum teres,
Prætextate, puellulæ ;
Jam cubile adeant viri.
Io Hymen Hymenæe, io!
    Io Hymen Hymenæe !   185
Vos bonæ, senibus viris
Cognitæ bene feminæ,
Collocate puellulam.
Io Hymen Hymenæe, io!
    Io Hymen Hymenæe!   190
Jam licet venias, marite :
Uxor in thalamo est tibi
Ore floridulo nitens ;

4

Alba parthenice velut,
    Luteumve papaver.   .   195
At marite (ita me juvent
Cœlites) nihilo minus
Pulcher es, neque te Venus
Negligit.   Sed abit dies:
    Perge; ne remorare.   200
Non diu remoratus es.
Jam venis.   Bona te Venus
Juverit, quoniam palam,
Quod cupis, capis, et bonum
    Non abscondis amorem.   205
Ille pulvis Erythrii,
Siderumque micantium,
Subducat numerum prius,
Qui vostri numerare volt
    Multa millia ludi.   210
Ludite, ut lubet, et brevi
Liberos date.   Non decet
Tam vetus sine liberis
Nomen esse, sed indidem
    Semper ingenerari.   215
Torquatus, volo, parvulus
Matris e gremio suæ
Porrigens teneras manus,
Dulce rideat ad patrem,

Semihiante labello.   220
Sit suo similis patri
Manlio, et facile insciis
Noscitetur ab omnibus ;
Et pudicitiam suæ
     Matris indicet ore.   225
Talis illius a bonâ
Matre laus genus approbet,
Qualis unica ab optimâ
Matre Telemacho manet
     Fama Penelopeo.   230
Claudite ostia, virgines :
Lusimus satis.   At, boni
Conjuges, bene vivite, et
Munere assiduo valentem
     Exercete juventam.   235

CARMEN XL.

Carmen Nuptiale.

Juvenes.

Vesper adest; juvenes, consurgite : Vesper
     Olympo
Exspectata diu vix tandem lumina tollit.
Surgere jam tempus, jam pingues linquere men-
    sas :

Jam veniet virgo ; jam dicetur Hymenæus.   4
Hymen o Hymenæe ! Hymen ades o Hymenæe !

Puellæ.

Cernitis, innuptæ, juvenes? consurgite contra,
Nimirum Œtæos ostendit Noctifer ignes.
Sic certe ; vide'n' ut perniciter exsiluêre?
Non temere exsiluêre : canent, quod visere par
    est.
Hymen o Hymenæe ! Hymen ades o Hyme-
    næe !   10

Juvenes.

Non facilis nobis, æquales, palma parata est :
Adspicite, innuptæ secum ut meditata requirunt.
Non frustra meditantur: habent, memorabile
    quod sit :
Nec mirum; totâ penitus quæ mente laborent.
Nos alio mentes, alio divisimus aures.   15
Jure igitur vincemur : amat victoria curam.
Quare nunc animos saltem committite vestros :
Dicere jam incipient, jam respondere decebit :
Hymen o Hymenæe ! Hymen ades o Hymenæe !

Puellæ.

Hespere, qui cœlo fertur crudelior ignis?   20
Qui natam possis complexu avellere matris,

Complexu matris retinentem avellere natam,
Et juveni ardenti castam donare puellam?
Quid faciant hostes captâ crudelius urbe?
Hymen o Hymenæe! Hymen ades o Hymenæe!

Juvenes.

Hespere, qui cœlo lucet jucundior ignis?   26
Qui desponsa tuâ firmes connubia flammâ,
[Quæ] pepigêre viri, pepigerunt ante parentes;
Nec junxêre prius quam se tuus extulit ardor.
Quid datur a Divis felici optatius horâ?   30
Hymen o Hymenæe! Hymen ades o Hymenæe!

Puellæ.

Hesperus e nobis, æquales, abstulit unam.

*   *   *   *   *

Namque tuo adventu vigilat custodia semper.
Nocte latent fures, quos idem sæpe, revertens,
Hespere, mutato comprendis nomine eosdem. 35

Juvenes.

*   *   *   *   *

At lubet innuptis ficto te carpere questu.
Quid tum si carpunt, tacitâ quem mente requi-
   runt?
Hymen o Hymenæe! Hymen ades o Hymenæe!

4 *

Puellæ.

Ut flos in septis secretus nascitur hortis,
Ignotus pecori, nullo contusus aratro,'   40
Quem mulcent auræ, firmat sol, educat imber:
Multi illum pueri, multæ optavêre puellæ :
Idem cum tenui carptus defloruit ungui,
Nulli illum pueri, nullæ optavêre puellæ :
Sic virgo, dum intacta manet, dum cara suis est. 45
Cum castum amisit polluto corpore florem,
Nec pueris jucunda manet, nec cara puellis.
Hymen o Hymenæe ! Hymen ades o Hymenæe !

Juvenes.

Ut vidua in nudo vitis quæ nascitur arvo,
Nunquam se extollit, nunquam mitem educat
     uvam ;   50
Sed, tenerum prono deflectens pondere corpus,
Jam jam contingit summum radice flagellum :
Hanc nulli agricolæ, nulli ac coluêre juvenci :
At, si forte eadem est ulmo conjúncta marito,
Multi illam agricolæ, multi ac coluêre juvenci : 55
Sic virgo, dum intacta manet, dum inculta senes-
     cit :
Cum par connubium maturo tempore adepta est,
Cara viro magis, et minus est invisa parenti.
Et tu ne pugna cum tali conjuge, virgo.

Non æquum est pugnare, pater quoi tradidit ipse,
Ipse pater cum matre, quibus parere necesse
    est. 61
Virginitas non tota tua est : ex parte parentûm est :
Tertia pars patri data, pars data tertia matri ;
Tertia sola tua est : noli pugnare duobus,
Qui genere sua jura simul cum dote dederunt. 65
Hymen o Hymenæe! Hymen ades o Hymenæe!

CARMEN XLI.

De Atye.

Super alta vectus Atys celeri rate maria,
Phrygium nemus citato cupide pede tetigit,
Adiitque opaca silvis redimita loca Deæ :
Stimulatus ubi furenti rabie, vagus animi,
Devolvit illa acutâ sibi pondera silice. 5
Itaque ut relicta sensit sibi membra sine viro,
Et jam recente terræ sola sanguine maculans,
Niveis citata cepit manibus leve typanum,
Typanum, tubam, Cybelle, tua, Mater, initia :
Quatiensque terga tauri teneris cava digitis, 10
Canere hæc suis adorta est tremebunda comitibus
  Agite, ite ad alta, Gallæ, Cybeles nemora simul
Simul ite, Dindymenæ dominæ vaga pecora,

Aliena quæ petentes, velut exsules, loca,   14
Sectam meam exsecutæ, duce me, mihi comites,
Rapidum salum tulistis, truculentaque pelagi,
Et corpus evirâstis Veneris nimio odio.
Hilarate heræ citatis erroribus animum.
Mora tarda mente cedat : simul ite, sequimini
Phrygiam ad domum Cybelles, Phrygia ad ne-
     mora Deæ,   20
Ubi cymbalûm sonat vox, ubi tympana reboant,
Tibicen ubi canit Phryx curvo grave calamo,
Ubi capita Mænades vi jaciunt hederigeræ,
Ubi sacra sancta acutis ululatibus agitant,
Ubi suevit illa Divæ volitare vaga cohors ;   25
Quo nos decet citatis celerare tripudiis.

  Simul hæc comitibus Atys cecinit, notha mulier,
Thiasus repente linguis trepidantibus ululat,
Leve tympanum remugit, cava cymbala recre-
     pant.   29
Viridem citus adit Idam properante pede chorus.
Furibunda simul, anhelans, vaga vadit, animi
     egens,
Comitata tympano Atys, per opacá nemora dux,
Veluti juvenca vitans onus indomita jugi.
Rapidæ ducem sequuntur Gallæ pede propero.
Itaque, ut domum Cybelles tetigêre, lassulæ   35
Nimio e labore, somnum capiunt sine Cerere.

Piger his labantes languore oculos sopor operit.
Abit in quiete molli rabidus furor animi.
Sed ubi oris aurei Sol radiantibus oculis   39
Lustravit æthera album, sola dura, mare ferum,
Pepulitque noctis umbras vegetis sonipedibus;
Ibi somnus excitum Atyn fugiens citus abiit:
Trepidantem 'eum recepit Dea Pasithea sinu.
Ita de quiete molli, rabidâ sine rabie,
Simul ipsa pectore Atys sua facta recoluit,   45
Liquidâque mente vidit sine quîs, ubique foret;
Animo æstuante rursum reditum ad vada tetulit:
Ibi maria vasta visens lacrymantibus oculis,
Patriam allocuta voce est ita mœsta miseriter:

    Patria o mea creatrix! patria o mea genitrix! 50
Ego quam miser relinquens, dominos ut herifugæ
Famuli solent, ad Idæ tetuli nemora pedem;
Ut apud nivem et ferarum gelida stabula forem,
Et earum omnia adirem furibunda latibula:
Ubinam, aut quibus locis te positam, patria, rear?
Cupit ipsa pupula ad te sibi dirigere aciem,   56
Rabie ferâ carens dum breve tempus animus est.
Egone a meâ remota hæc ferar in nemora domo?
Patriâ, bonis, amicis, genitoribus abero?
Abero foro, palæstrâ, stadio et gymnasiis?   60
Miser, ah miser, querendum est etiam atque
    etiam, anime.

Quod enim genus figuræ est, ego non quod ha-
    buerim ?
Ego puber, ego adolescens, ego ephebus, ego puer,
Ego gymnasî fui flos ; ego eram decus olei.
Mihi januæ frequentes, mihi limina tepida,   65
Mihi floridis corollis redimita domus erat,
Linquendum ubi esset orto mihi sole cubiculum.
Egone Deûm ministra, et Cybeles famula ferar ?
Ego Mænas, ego mei pars, ego vir sterilis ero ?
Ego viridis algida Idæ nive amicta loca colam? 70
Ego vitam agam sub altis Phrygiæ columinibus,
Ubi cerva silvicultrix, ubi aper nemorivagus ?
Jam jam dolet, quod egi, jam jamque pœnitet.

    Roseis ut huic labellis palans sonitus abiit, 74
Geminas Deorum ad aures nova nuntia referens,
Ibi juncta juga resolvens Cybele leonibus,
Lævumque pecoris hostem stimulans, ita loquitur:
Agedum, inquit, age ferox, i : face ut hinc, furo-
    ribus,
Face ut hinc, furoris ictu, reditum in nemora
    ferat,
Mea libere nimis qui fugere imperia cupit.   80
Age, cæde terga caudâ : tua verbera patere :
Face cuncta mugienti fremitu loca retonent :
Rutilam ferox torosâ cervice quate jubam.

    Ait hæc minax Cybelle, religatque juga manu.

Ferus, ipse sese adhortans, rapidum incitat an-
    imum : 85
Vadit, fremit, refringit virgulta pede vago.
At ubi ultima albicantis loca litoris adiit,
Tenerumque vidit Atyn prope marmora pelagi,
Facit impetum. Ille demens fugit in nemora fera.
Ibi semper omne vitæ spatium famula fuit. 90
    Dea, magna Dea, Cybelle, Didymi Dea domina,
Procul a meâ tuus sit furor omnis, hera, domo :
Alios age incitatos, alios age rabidos.

CARMEN XLII.

Nuptiæ Pelei et Thetidos.

Peliaco quondam prognatæ vertice pinus
Dicuntur liquidas Neptuni nâsse per undas
Phasidos ad fluctus, et fines Æetæos ;
Cum lecti juvenes, Argivæ robora pubis,
Auratam optantes Colchis avertere pellem, 5
Ausi sunt vada salsa citâ decurrere puppi,
Cœrula verrentes abiegnis æquora palmis ;
Diva quibus, retinens in summis urbibus arces,
Ipsa levi fecit volitantem flamine currum,
Pinea conjungens inflexæ texta carinæ. 10
Illa rudem cursu prima imbuit Amphitrite-

Quæ simul ac rostro ventosum proscidit æquor,
Tortaque remigio spumis incanduit unda ;
Emersêre feri candenti e gurgite vultus,
Æquoreæ monstrum Nereïdes admirantes ;   15
Illâque, haudque aliâ, viderunt luce marinas
Mortales oculi nudato corpore nymphas,
Nutricum tenus exstantes e gurgite cano.
Tum Thetidis Peleus incensus fertur amore : 19
Tum Thetis humanos non despexit hymenæos :
Tum Thetidi pater ipse jugandum Pelea sensit.
O nimis optato sæclorum tempore nati
Heroës, salvete, Deûm genus ! o bona mater !
Vos ego sæpe meo vos carmine compellabo.
Teque adeo eximie tædis felicibus aucte,   25
Thessaliæ columen, Peleu, quoi Jupiter ipse,
Ipse suos Divûm genitor concessit amores.
Tene Thetis tenuit pulcherrima Neptunine ?
Tene suam Tethys concessit ducere neptem,
Oceanusque, mari totum qui amplectitur orbem ?
Quæ simul optatæ finito tempore luces   31
Advenêre, domum conventu tota frequentat
Thessalia : oppletur lætanti regia cœtu :
Dona ferunt : præ se declarant gaudia vultu.
Deseritur Scyros : linquunt Phthiotica Tempe,
Cranonisque domos, ac mœnia Larissæa :   36
Pharsaliam coëunt, Pharsalia tecta frequentant.

Rura colit nemo : mollescunt colla juvencis :
Non humilis curvis purgatur vinea rastris :
Non glebam prono convellit vomere taurus :　40
Non falx attenuat frondatorum arboris umbram :
Squalida desertis robigo infertur aratris.

　Ipsius at sedes (quâcumque opulenta recessit
Regia) fulgenti splendent auro, atque argento.
Candet ebur soliis ; collucent pocula mensis :　45
Tota domus gaudet regali splendida gazâ.
Pulvinar vero Divæ geniale locatur
Sedibus in mediis, Indo quod dente politum
Tincta tegit roseo conchylî purpura fuco.
Hæc vestis, priscis hominum variata figuris,　50
Heroum mirâ virtutes indicat arte.
Namque fluentisono prospectans litore Diæ
Thesea cedentem celeri cum classe tuetur
Indomitos in corde gerens Ariadna furores :
Necdum etiam sese, quæ visit, visere credit ;　55
Utpote fallaci quæ tum primum excita somno
Desertam in solâ miseram se cernit arenâ.
Immemor at juvenis fugiens pellit vada remis,
Irrita ventosæ linquens promissa procellæ :
Quem procul ex algâ mœstis Minoïs ocellis,　60
Saxea ut effigies bacchantis prospicit Euœ,
Prospicit, et magnis curarum fluctuat undis,
Non flavo retinens subtilem vertice mitram

5

Non contecta levi velatum pectus amictu,
Non tereti strophio luctantes vincta papillas ; 65
Omnia quæ, toto delapsa e corpore passim,
Ipsius ante pedes, fluctus salis alludebant.
Sed neque tum mitræ, neque tum fluitantis amictûs
Illa vicem curans, toto ex te pectore, Theseu,
Toto animo, totâ pendebat perdita mente.   70
Ah misera! assiduis quam luctibus externavit
Spinosas Erycina serens in pectore curas
Illâ tempestate, ferox quo tempore Theseus,
Egressus curvis e litoribus Piræei,
Attigit injusti regis Gortynia tecta.   75
Nam perhibent, olim, crudeli peste coactam
Androgeoneæ pœnas exsolvere cædis,
Electos juvenes simul, et decus innuptarum,
Cecropiam solitam esse dapem dare Minotauro :
Quîs angusta malis cum mœnia vexarentur,   80
Ipse suum Theseus pro caris corpus Athenis
Projicere optavit potius, quam talia Cretam
Funera Cecropiæ ne-funera portarentur.
Atque ita nave levi nitens ac lenibus auris,
Magnanimum ad Minoa venit, sedesque superbas.
Hunc simul ac cupido conspexit lumine virgo 86
Regia, quam suaves exspirans castus odores
Lectulus in molli complexu matris alebat ;

(Quales Eurotæ progignunt flumina myrtos,
Aurave distinctos educit verna colores)   90
Non prius ex illo flagrantia declinavit
Lumina, quam cuncto concepit pectore flammam
Funditus, atque imis exarsit tota medullis.
Heu! misere exagitans immiti corde furores,
Sancte puer, curis hominum qui gaudia mis-
  ces,   95
Quæque regis Golgos, quæque Idalium fron-
  dosum, .
Qualibus incensam jactâstis mente puellam
Fluctibus, in flavo sæpe hospite suspirantem!
Quantos illa tulit languenti corde timores!
Quantum sæpe magis fulgore expalluit auri! 100
Cum, sævum cupiens contra contendere mon-
  strum,   .
Aut mortem oppeterit Theseus, aut præmia
  laudis.
Non ingrata, tamen frustra, munuscula Divis
Promittens, tacito suspendit vota labello.
Nam, velut in summo quatientem brachia
  Tauro   105
Quercum, aut conigeram sudanti corpore pinum,
Indomitus turbo, contorquens flamine robur,
Eruit; illa procul, radicibus exturbata,
Prona cadit, lateque et comminus obvia frangens;

Sic domito sævum prostravit corpore Theseus 110
Nequidquam vanis jactantem cornua ventis.
Inde pedem sospes multâ cum laude reflexit,
Errabunda regens tenui vestigia filo ;
Ne labyrintheis e flexibus egredientem
Tecti frustraretur inobservabilis error.   115
Sed quid ego, a primo digressus carmine, plura
Commemorem? ut linquens genitoris filia vultum,
Ut consanguineæ complexum, ut denique matris,
[Quæ misera in natâ flevit deperdita,] læta
Omnibus his Thesei dulcem præoptârit amorem?
Aut ut vecta ratis spumosa ad litora Diæ?   121
Aut ut eam, tristi devinctam lumina somno,
Liquerit immemori discedens pectore conjux ?
Sæpe illam perhibent ardenti corde furentem
Clarisonas imo fudisse e pectore voces,   125
Ac tum præruptos tristem conscendere montes,
Unde aciem in pelagi vastos protenderet æstus ;
Tum tremuli salis adversas procurrere in undas,
Mollia nudatæ tollentem tegmina suræ ;
Atque hæc extremis mœstam dixisse querelis, 130
Frigidulos udo singultus ore cientem :

Siccine me, patriis avectam, perfide, ab oris,
Perfide, deserto liquisti in litore, Theseu ?
Siccine, discedens, neglecto numine Divûm,
Immemor, ah! devota domum perjuria portas? 135

Nullane res potuit crudelis flectere mentis
Consilium? tibi nulla fuit clementia præsto,
Immite ut nostri vellet [miserescere] pectus?
At non hæc quondam nobis promissa dedisti
Voce: mihi non hoc miseræ sperare jubebas; 140
Sed connubia læta, sed optatos hymenæos;
Quæ cuncta aërii discerpunt irrita venti.
Jam jam nulla viro juranti femina credat;
Nulla viri speret sermones esse fideles:
Qui, dum aliquid cupiens animus prægestit
 apisci, 145
Nil metuunt jurare, nihil promittere parcunt:
Sed, simul ac cupidæ mentis satiata libido est,
Dicta nihil metuêre, nihil perjuria curant.
Certe ego te in medio versantem turbine leti
Eripui, et potius germanum amittere crevi, 150
Quam tibi fallaci supremo in tempore deessem.
Pro quo, dilaceranda feris dabor alitibusque
Præda; neque injectâ tumulabor mortua terrâ.
Quænam te genuit solâ sub rupe leæna?
Quod mare conceptum spumantibus exspuit
 undis? 155
Quæ Syrtis, quæ Scylla vorax, quæ vasta
 Charybdis,
Talia qui reddis pro dulci præmia vitâ?
Si tibi non cordi fuerant connubia nostra,
 5 *

Sæva quod horrebas prisci præcepta parentis;
Attamen in vestras potuisti ducere sedes,   160
Quæ tibi jucundo famularer serva labore,
Candida permulcens liquidis vestigia lymphis,
Purpureave tuum consternens veste cubile. «
Sed quid ego ignaris nequidquam conqueror
     auris,
Externata malo, quæ, nullis sensibus auctæ,   165
Nec missas audire queunt, nec reddere voces?
Ille autem prope jam mediis versatur in undis;
Nec quisquam apparet vacuâ mortalis in algâ.
Sic, nimis insultans extremo tempore, sæva
Fors etiam nostris invidit questibus aures.   170
Jupiter omnipotens! utinam ne tempore primo
Gnosia Cecropiæ tetigissent litora puppes;
Indomito nec dira ferens stipendia tauro
Perfidus in Creta religasset navita funem; ·
Nec malus hic, celans dulci crudelia formâ   175
Consilia, in nostris requiêsset sedibus hospes!
Nam quo me referam? quaii spe perdita nitar?
[Idomeniosne] petam montes? at, gurgite lato
Discernens, ponti truculentum dividit æquor.
Au patris auxilium sperem? quemne ipsa reliqui,
Respersum juvenem fraternâ cæde secuta?   181
Conjugis an fido consoler memet amore?
Quine fugit lentos incurvans gurgite remos?

Præterea litus, nullo sola insula tecto :
Nec patet egressus, pelagi cingentibus undis. 185
Nulla fugæ ratio ; nulla spes : omnia muta,
Omnia sunt deserta : ostentant omnia letum.
Non tamen ante mihi languescent lumina morte,
Nec prius a fesso secedent corpore sensus,   189
Quam justam a Divis exposcam prodita multam,
Cœlestûmque fidem postremâ comprecer horâ.
Quare, facta virûm multantes vindice pœnâ,
Eumenides, quibus anguineo redimita capillo
Frons exspirantes præportat pectoris iras,
Huc huc adventate, meas audite querelas,   195
Quas ego (væ miseræ !) extremis proferre me-
    dullis
Cogor, inops, ardens, amenti cæca furore.
Quæ quoniam vere nascuntur pectore ab imo,
Vos nolite pati nostrum vanescere luctum :
Sed, quali solam Theseus me mente reliquit, 200
Tali mente, Deæ, funestet seque suosque.

    Has postquam mœsto profudit pectore voces,
Supplicium sævis exposcens anxia factis ;
Annuit invicto Cœlestûm numine rector ;   204
Quo tunc et tellus, atque horrida contremuerunt
Æquora, concussitque micantia sidera mundus.
Ipse autem cæcâ mentem caligine Theseus
Consitus, oblito dimisit pectore cuncta,

Quæ mandata prius constanti mente tenebat :
Dulcia nec mæsto sustollens signa parenti, 210
Sospitem et ereptum se ostendit visere portum.
Namque ferunt, olim classi cum, mœnia Divæ
Linquentem, natum ventis concrederet Ægeus,
Talia complexum juveni mandata dedisse :

Nate, mihi longâ jucundior unice vitâ, 215
Nate, ego quem in dubios cogor dimittere casus,
Reddite in extremæ nuper mihi fine senectæ,
Quandoquidem fortuna mea, ac tua fervida virtus
Eripit invito mihi te, quoi languida nondum
Lumina sunt nati carâ saturata figurâ ; 220
Non ego te gaudens lætanti pectore mittam,
Nec te ferre sinam Fortunæ signa secundæ :
Sed primum multas expromam mente quere-
    las,
Canitiem terrâ atque infuso pulvere fœdans :
Inde infecta vago suspendam lintea malo, 225
Nostros ut luctus, nostræque incendia mentis,
Carbasus obscurâ dicat ferrugine Ibera.
Quod tibi si sancti concesserit incola Itoni,
(Quæ nostrum genus ac sedes defendere fretis
Annuit) ut tauri respergas sanguine dextram ; 230
Tum vero facito, ut memori tibi condita corde
Hæc vigeant mandata ; nec ulla obliteret ætas :
Ut, simul ac nostros invisent lumina colles,

Funestam antennæ deponant undique vestem,
Candidaque intorti sustollant vela rudentes, 235
[Lucida quâ splendent summi carchesia mali :]
Quamprimum cernens ut lætâ gaudia mente
Agnoscam, cum te reducem ætas prospera sistet.

Hæc mandata prius constanti mente tenentem
Thesea, ceu pulsæ ventorum flamine nubes 240
Aërium nivei montis, liquêre, cacumen.
At pater, ut summâ prospectum ex arce petebat,
Anxia in assiduos absumens lumina fletus,
Cum primum inflati conspexit lintea veli,
Præcipitem sese scopulorum e vertice jecit, 245
Amissum credens immiti Thesea fato.
Sic, funesta domûs ingressus tecta paternâ
Morte, ferox Theseus, qualem Minoïdi luctum
Obtulerat, mente immemori talem ipse recepit.
Quæ tum prospectans cedentem mœsta cari-
    nam, 250
Multiplices animo volvebat saucia curas.
At parte ex aliâ florens volitabat Iacchus,
Cum thiaso Satyrorum, et Nysigenis Silenis,
Te quærens, Ariadna, tuoque incensus amore; 254
Qui tum alacres passim lymphatâ mente furebant,
Euœ bacchantes, Euœ, capita inflectentes.
Horum pars tectâ quatiebant cuspide thyrsos ;
Pars e divulso raptabant membra juvenco ;

Pars sese tortis serpentibus incingebant;
Pars obscura cavis celebrabant orgia cistis,   260
Orgia, quæ frustra cupiunt audire profani :
Plangebant alii proceris tympana palmis,
Aut tereti tenues tinnitus ære ciebant.
Multis raucisonos efflabant cornua bombos,
Barbaraque horribili stridebat tibia cantu.   265
    Talibus amplifice vestis decorata figuris
Pulvinar complexa suo velabat amictu.
Quæ postquam cupide spectando Thessala pubes
Expleta est, sanctis cœpit decedere Divis.
Hîc qualis flatu placidum mare matutino   270
Horrificans Zephyrus proclivas incitat undas,
Aurorâ exoriente, vagi sub lumina solis;
Quæ tarde primum clementi flamine pulsæ
Procedunt, leni resonant plangore cachinni :
Post, vento crescente, magis magis increbre-
      scunt,   275
Purpureâque procul nantes a luce refulgent :
Sic tum vestibuli linquentes regia tecta,
Ad se quisque vago passim pede discedebant.
Quorum post abitum, princeps e vertice Pelî
Advenit Chiron portans silvestria dona :   280
Nam quotcumque ferunt campi, quos Thessala
      magnis
Montibus ora creat, quos propter fluminis undas

Aura parit flores tepidi fecunda Favoni,
Hos indistinctis plexos tulit ipse corollis,
Quîs permulsa domus jucundo risit odore. 285
Confestim Peneos adest, viridantia Tempe,
Tempe, quæ silvæ cingunt superimpendentes,
Mnemonidum, linquens, doctis celebranda cho-
    reis,
Non vacuus: namque ille tulit radicitus altas
Fagos, ac recto proceras stipite laurus, 290
Non sine nutanti platano, lentâque sorore
Flammati Phaëthontis, et aëriâ cupressu :
Hæc circum sedes late contexta locavit,
Vestibulum ut molli velatum fronde vireret.
Post hunc consequitur sollerti corde Prometheus,
Extenuata gerens veteris vestigia pœnæ ; 296
Quam quondam, silici restrictus membra catenâ,
Persolvit, pendens e verticibus præruptis.
Inde pater Divûm, sanctâ cum conjuge, natisque
Advenit cœlo, te solum, Phœbe, relinquens, 300
Unigenamque simul cultricem montibus Idri :
Pelea nam, tecum pariter, soror adspernata est,
Nec Thetidis tædas voluit celebrare jugales.
Qui postquam niveos flexerunt sedibus artus,
Large multiplici constructæ sunt dape mensæ ; 305
Cum iterea, infirmo quatientes corpora motu,
Veridicos Parcæ cœperunt edere cantus.

His corpus ~~~~ undique quer-
   cus,
Candida purpureâ ~ uxerat orâ :
At roseo niveæ resideba· tæ,
Æternumque manus carpe aborem.
Læva colum molli lanâ retineba ttum :
Dextera tum leviter deducens fil his
Formabat digitis; tum prono in p torquens
Libratum tereti versabat turbine fusum :   315
Atque ita decerpens æquabat semper opus dens ;
Laneaque aridulis hærebant morsa labellis,
Quæ prius in levi fuerant exstantia filo.
Ante pedes autem candentis mollia lanæ
Vellera virgati custodibant calathisci.   320
Hæ tum clarisonâ pellentes vellera voce,
Talia divino fuderunt carmine fata,
Carmine, perfidiæ quod post nulla arguet ætas :

  O decus eximium, magnis virtutibus augens,
Emathiæ tutamen opis, clarissime nato !   325
Accipe, quod lætâ tibi pandunt luce sorores,
Veridicum oraclum: sed vos, quæ fata sequuntur,
Currite, ducentes subtemina, currite, fusi.

  Adveniet tibi jam portans optata maritis
Hesperus: adveniet fausto cum sidere conjux, 330
Quæ tibi flexanimo mentem perfundat amore,
Languidulosque paret tecum conjungere somnos,

Levia substernens robusto brachia collo.
Currite, ducentes subtemina, currite, fusi.

Nulla domus tales unquam contexit amores : 335
Nullus amor tali conjunxit fœdere amantes,
Qualis adest Thetidi, qualis concordia Peleo.
Currite, ducentes subtemina, currite, fusi.

Nascetur vobis expers terroris Achilles,
Hostibus haud tergo, sed forti pectore, notus : 340
Qui, persæpe vago victor certamine cursûs,
Flammea prævertet celeris vestigia cervæ.
Currite, ducentes subtemina, currite, fusi.

Non illi quisquam bello se conferet heros,
Cum Phrygii Teucro manabunt sanguine rivi ; 345
Troïcaque obsidens longinquo mœnia bello
Perjuri Pelopis vastabit tertius hæres.
Currite, ducentes subtemina, currite, fusi.

Illius egregias virtutes, claraque facta,
Sæpe fatebuntur natorum in funere matres ; 350
Cum in cinerem canos solvent a vertice crines,
Putridaque infirmis variabunt pectora palmis.
Currite, ducentes subtemina, currite, fusi.

Namque, velut densas prosternens cultor aris-
    tas,
Sole sub ardenti flaventia demetit arva,   355
Trojugenûm infesto prosternet corpora ferro.
Currite, ducentes subtemina, currite, fusi.

6

Testis erit magnis virtutibus unda Scamandri,
Quæ passim rapido diffunditur Hellesponto :
Quojus iter cæsis angustans corporum acer-
    vis,   .   360
Alta tepefaciet permixtâ flumina cæde.
Currite, ducentes subtemina, currite, fusi.

    Denique testis erit morti quoque dedita præda,
Cum teres, excelso coacervatum aggere, bustum
Excipiet niveos perculsæ virginis artus.   .   365
Currite, ducentes subtemina, currite, fusi.

    Nam, simul ac fessis dederit fors copiam
      Achivis
Urbis Dardaniæ Neptunia solvere vincla,
Alta Polyxeniâ madefient cæde sepulcra ;
Quæ, velut ancipiti succumbens victima ferro, 370
Projiciet truncum submisso poplite corpus.
Currite, ducentes subtemina, currite, fusi.

    Quare agite, optatos animi conjungite amores ;
Accipiat conjux felici fœdere Divam :
Dedatur cupido jamdudum nupta marito.   375
Currite, ducentes subtemina, currite, fusi.

    Non illam nutrix orienti luce revisens,
Hesterno collum poterit circumdare filo.
Currite, ducentes subtemina, currite, fusi.

    Anxia nec mater, discordis mœsta puellæ   380
Secubitu, caros mittet sperare nepotes.

Currite, ducentes subtemina, currite, fusi.

Talia profantes quondam, felicia Pelei
Carmina divino cecinerunt omine Parcæ.
Præsentes namque ante domos invisere castas 385
Sæpius, et sese mortali ostendere cœtû,
Cœlicolæ, nondum spretâ pietate, solebant.
Sæpe pater Divûm templo in fulgente revisens,
Annua cum festis venissent sacra diebus,
Conspexit terrâ centum procurrere curras. 390
Sæpe vagus Liber Parnassi vertice summo
Thyadas effusis euantes crinibus egit :
Cum Delphi totâ certatim ex urbe ruentes
Acciperent læti Divum fumantibus aris. ·
Sæpe in letifero belli certamine Mavors, 395
Aut rapidi Tritonis hera, aut Rhamnusia virgo,
Armatas hominum est præsens hortata catervas.
Sed, postquam tellus scelere est imbuta nefando,
Justitiamque omnes cupidâ de mente fugârunt ;
Perfudêre manus fraterno sanguine fratres ; 400
Destitit exstinctos natus lugere parentes ;
Optavit genitor primævi funera nati,
Liber ut innuptæ poteretur flore novercæ ;
Ignaro mater substernens se impia nato,
Impia non verita est Divos scelerare penates ; 405
Omnia fanda, nefanda, malo permixta furore,
Justificam nobis mentem avertêre Deorum.

Quare nec tales dignantur visere cœtus,
Nec se contingi patiuntur lumine claro.

CARMEN XLIII.

Ad Hortalum.

Etsi me assiduo confectum cura dolore
    Sevocat a doctis, Hortale, virginibus;
Nec potis est dulces Musarum expromere fetus
    Mens animi; tantis fluctuat ipsa malis;
Namque mei nuper Lethæo gurgite fratris   5
    Pallidulum manans alluit unda pedem;
Troïa Rhœteo quem subter litore tellus
    Ereptum nostris obterit ex oculis.
[Alloquar? audierone unquam tua facta loquen-
    tem?]
Nunquam ego te, vitâ frater amabilior,   10
Adspiciam posthac? At certe semper amabo;
    Semper mœsta tuâ carmina morte canam;
Qualia sub densis ramorum concinit umbris
    Daulias, absumti fata gemens Ityli.
Sed tamen in tantis mœroribus, Hortale, mitto 15
    Hæc expressa tibi carmina Battiadæ;
Ne tua dicta vagis nequidquam credita ventis
    Effluxisse meo forte putes animo;

Ut missum sponsi furtivo munere malum
    Procurrit casto virginis e gremio,   20
Quod, miseræ oblitæ molli sub veste locatum,
    Dum adventu matris prosilit, excutitur;
Atque illud prono præceps agitur decursu;
    Huic manat tristi conscius ore rubor.

CARMEN XLIV.

De Comâ Berenices.

Omnia qui magni dispexit lumina mundi,
    Qui stellarum ortus comperit atque obitus;
Flammeus ut rapidi solis nitor obscuretur;
    Ut cedant certis sidera temporibus;
Ut Triviam furtim sub Latmia saxa relegans, 5
    Dulcis amor gyro devocet aërio;
Idem me ille Conon cœlesti lumine vidit
    E Bereniceo vertice cæsariem
Fulgentem clare: quam multis illa Deorum,
    Levia protendens brachia, pollicita est; 10
Quâ rex tempestate, novo auctus hymenæo,
    Vastatum fines iverat Assyrios.

       *   *   *   *   *
       *   *   *   *   *

6 *

Estne novis nuptis odio Venus? anne paren-
    tûm   15
  Frustrantur falsis gaudia lacrymulis,
Ubertim thalami quas intra limina fundunt?
  Non, ita me Divi, véra gemunt, juerint.
Id mea me multis docuit regina querelis,
  Invisente novo prœlia torva viro.   20
Ut tu nunc orbum luxti deserta cubile,
  Et fratris cari flebile discidium!
Quam penitus mœstas exedit cura medullas!
  Ut tibi nunc toto pectore sollicitæ
Sensibus ereptis mens excidit! Atqui ego
    certe   25
  Cognôram a parvâ virgine magnanimam.
Anne bonum oblita es facinus, quo regium adep-
    ta es
  Conjugium, quod non fortior ausit alis?
Sed tum, mœsta virum mittens, quæ verba locu-
    ta es!
  Jupiter! ut trîsti lumina sæpe manu!   30
Quis te mutavit tantus Deus? an quod amantes
  Non longe a caro corpore abesse volunt?
Atque ibi me cunctis pro dulci conjuge Divis,
  Non sine taurino sanguine, pollicita es,   34
Si reditum tetulisset is haud in tempore longo, et
  Captam Asiam Ægypti finibus adjiceret.

Quîs ego pro factis cœlesti reddita cœtû,
    Pristina vota novo munere dissolüo.
Invita, o regina, tuo de vertice cessi,
    Invita : adjuro teque tuumque caput ;   40
Digna ferat, quod siquis inaniter adjurârit.
    Sed qui se ferro postulet esse parem ?
Ille quoque eversus mons est, quem maximum
    in oris
    Progenies Thiæ clara supervehitur,
Cum Medi peperêre novum mare, cumque juven-
    tus   45
    Per medium classi barbara navit Athon.
Quid facient crines, cum ferro talia cedant ?
    Jupiter ! ut Chalybôn omne genus pereat ;
Et qui principio sub terrâ quærere venas
    Institit, ac ferri fingere duritiem !   50
Abjunctæ paulo ante comæ mea fata sorores
    Lugebant, cum se Memnonis Æthiopis
Unigena, impellens nutantibus aëra pennis,
    Obtulit Arsinoës Chloridos ales equus ;
Isque per ætherias me tollens advolat auras,   55
    Et Veneris casto collocat in gremio.
Ipsa suum Zephyritis eo famulum legârat,
    Grata Canopæis incola litoribus.
Scilicet in vario ne solum limite cœli
    Ex Ariadneis aurea temporibus   60

Fixa corona foret; sed nos quoque fulgeremus
    Devotæ flavi verticis exuviæ.
Uvidulam a fletu, cedentem ad templa Deûm, me
    Sidus in antiquis Diva novum posuit.
Virginis et sævi contingens namque Leonis   65
    Lumina, Callisto juncta Lycaoniæ
Vertor in occasum, tardum dux ante Booten,
    Qui vix sero alto mergitur Oceano.
Sed, quamquam me nocte premunt vestigia Di-
    vûm,
    Luce autem canæ Tethyi restituor;   70
(Pace tuâ fari hæc liceat, Rhamnusia virgo;
    Namque ego non ullo vera timore tegam;
Non, si me infestis discerpant sidera dictis,
    Condita quin veri pectoris evolüam)
Non his tam lætor rebus, quam me abfore sem-
    per,   75
    Abfore me a dominæ vertice, discrucior :
Quîcum ego, dum virgo quondam fuit, omnibus
    [explens]
    Unguentis, unâ millia multa bibi.
Nunc vos, optato quas junxit lumine tæda,
    Non prius unanimis corpora conjugibus   80
Tradite, nudantes rejectâ veste papillas,
    Quam jucunda mihi munera libet onyx;
Vester onyx, casto petitis quæ jura cubili.

Sed, quæ se impuro dedit adulterio,
Illius, ah! mala dona levis bibat irrita pulvis: 85
  Namque ego ab indignis præmia nulla peto.
Sic magis, o nuptæ, semper concordia vestras,
  Semper amor sedes incolat assiduus.
Tu vero, regina, tuens cum sidera, Divam
  Placabis festis luminibus Venerem   90
Sanguinis expertem, non votis esse tuam me,
  Sed potius largis effice muneribus.
Sidera cur retinent? utinam coma regia fiam:
  Proximus Hydrochöei fulguret Oarion.

CARMEN XLV.

Ad Manlium.

Quod mihi, fortunâ casuque oppressus acerbo, 1?.
  Conscriptum hoc lacrymis mittis epistolium,
Naufragum ut ejectum spumantibus æquoris un-
    dis
  Sublevem, et a mortis limine restituam;
Quem neque sancta Venus molli requiescere
    somno   5
  Desertum in lecto cœlibe perpetitur;
Nec veterum dulci scriptorum carmine Musæ
  Oblectant, cum mens anxia pervigilat:

Id gratum est mihi, me quoniam tibi ducis ami-
    cum,
  Muneraque et Musarum hinc petis et Ven-
    eris.   10
Sed tibi ne mea sint ignota incommoda, Manli,
  Neu me odisse putes hospitis officium ;
Accipe, quîs merser fortunæ fluctibus ipse,
  Ne amplius a misero dona beata petas.
Tempore quo primum vestis mihi tradita pura est,
  Jucundum cum ætas florida ver ageret,   16
Multa satis lusi : non est Dea nescia nostri,
  Quæ dulcem curis miscet amaritiem.
Sed totum hoc studium luctu fraterna mihi mors
  Abstulit.   O misero frater ademte mihi !   20
Tu mea, tu moriens fregisti commoda, frater :
  Tecum unâ tota est nostra sepulta domus :
Omnia tecum unâ perierunt gaudia nostra,
  Quæ tuus in vitâ dulcis alebat amor.
Quojus ego interitu totâ de mente fugavi   25
  Hæc studia, atque omnes delicias animi.
      *   *   *   *   *
      *   *   *   *   *

Ignosces igitur, si, quæ mihi luctus ademit,
  Hæc tibi non tribuo munera, cum nequeo. 30
Nam, quod scriptorum non magna est copia
    apud me,

Hoc fit, quod Romæ vivimus : illa domus ;
Illa mihi sedes, illic mea carpitur ætas :
 Huc una ex multis capsula me sequitur.
Quod cum ita sit, nolim statuas, nos mente ma-
  ligna   35
 Id facere, aut animo non satis ingenuo,
Quod tibi uon utriusque petiti copia facta est :
 Ultro ego deferrem, copia siqua foret.
Non possum reticere, Deæ, quâ Manlius in re
 Juverit, aut quantis juverit officiis ;   40
Ne fugiens sæclis obliviscentibus ætas
 Illius hoc eæcâ nocte tegat studium.
Sed dicam vobis.   Vos porro dicite multis
 Millibus, et facite hæc charta loquatur anus.
    ·   *   *   *   *   *   45
 Notescatque magis mortuus, atque magis ;
Ne tenuem texens sublimis aranea telam,
 Deserto in Manlî nomine opus faciat.
Nam, mihi quam dederit duplex Amathusia cu-
  ram,
 Scitis, et in quo me corruerit genere.   50
Cum tantum arderem, quantum Trinaòria rupes,
 Lymphaque in Œtæis Malia Thermopylis ;
Mœsta neque assiduo tabescere lumina fletu
 Cessarent, tristique imbre madere genæ ;
Qualis in aërii pellucens vertice montis   55

Rivus muscoso prosilit e lapide ;
Qui, cum de pronâ præceps est valle volutus,
   Per medium densi transit iter populi,
Dulce viatori lasso in sudore levamen,
   Cum gravis exustos æstus hiulcat agros :   60
Ac veluti nigro jactatis turbine nautis
   Lenius adspirans aura secunda venit, ⸱
Jam prece Pollucis, jam Castoris, imploratâ :
   Tale fuit nobis Manlius auxilium.
Is clausum lato patefecit limite campum,   65
   Isque domum nobis, isque dedit dominam,
Ad quam communes exerceremus amores,
   Quo mea se molli candida Diva pede
Intulit, et trito fulgentem in limine plantam
   Innixa, argutâ constitit in soleâ :   70
Conjugis ut quondam flagrans advenit amore,
   Protesilaëam Laodamia domum
Inceptam frustra, nondum cum sanguine sacro
   Hostia coelestes pacificâsset heros.
Nil mihi tam valde placeat, Rhamnusia virgo, 75
   Quod temere invitis suscipiatur heris.
Quam jejuna pium desideret ara cruorem,
   Docta est amisso Laodamia viro ;
Conjugis ante coacta novi dimittere collum,
   Quam veniens una atque altera rursus
     hiems   80

Noctibus in longis avidum saturâsset amorem,
  Posset ut abrupto vivere conjugio ;
Quod scibant Parcæ non longo tempore abesse,
  Si miles muros îsset ad Iliacos.
Nam tum Helenæ raptu primores Argivorum 85
  Cœperat ad sese Troja ciere viros :
Troja nefas, commune sepulcrum Europæ Asi-
    æque,
  Troja virûm et virtutum omnium acerba
    cinis ;
Quæ nempe et nostro letum miserabile fratri
  Attulit : hei misero frater ademte mihi ! 90
Hei misero fratri jucundum lumen'ademtum !
  Tecum unâ tota est nostra sepulta domus :
Omnia tecum unâ perierunt gaudia nostra,
  Quæ tuus in vitâ dulcis alebat amor :
Quem nunc tam longe, non inter nota sepulcra, 95
  Nec prope cognatos compositum cineres,
Sed Trojâ obscœnâ, Trojâ infelice sepultum,
  Detinet extremo terra aliena solo :
Ad quam tum properans fertur simul undique
    pubes
  Græcâ penetrales deseruisse focos ; 100
Ne Paris abductâ gavisus libera mœchâ
  Otia pacato degeret in thalamo.
Quo tibi tum casu, pulcherrima Laodamia,

7

Ereptum est vitâ dulcius atque animâ.
Conjugium ; tanto te absorbens vortice amoris 105
  Æstus in abruptum detulerat barathrum ;
Quale ferunt Graii Pheneum prope Cylleneum
  . Siccare emulsâ pingue palude solum ;
Quod quondam cæsis montis fodisse medullis
  Audit falsiparens Amphitryoniades,   110
Tempore quo certâ Stymphalia monstra sagittâ
  Perculit, imperio deterioris heri ;
Pluribus ut cœli tereretur janua Divis,
  Hebe nec longâ virginitate foret.
Sed tuus altus amor barathro fuit altior illo, 115
  Qui tunc indomitam ferre jugum docuit.
Nam neque tam carum confecto ætate parenti
  Una caput seri nata nepotis alit :
Qui, cum divitiis vix tandem inventus avitis
  Nomen testatas intulit in tabulas,   120
Impia derisi gentilis gaudia tollens,
  Suscitat a cano volturium capite.
Nec tantum niveo gavisa est ulla columbo
  Compar, quæ multo dicitur improbius
Oscula mordenti semper decerpere rostro ; 125
  Quamquam præcipue multivola est mulier.
Sed tu horum magnos vicisti sola furores,
  Ut semel es flavo conciliata viro ;
Aut nihil, aut paulo quoi tum concedere digna,

Lux mea se nostrum contulit in gremium. . 130
Quam circumcursans hinc illinc sæpè Cupido
Fulgebat crocinâ candidus in tunicâ.

* * * * * * *

Hoc tibi, quod potui, confectum carmine munus
  Pro multis, Manli, redditur officiis,
Ne vostrum scabrâ tangat robigine nomen   150
  Hæc atque illa dies, atque alia, atque alia.
Huc addent Divi quam plurima, quæ Themis olim
  Antiquis solita est munera ferre piis.
Sitis felices et tu simul et tua vita,
  Et domus ipsa, in quâ lusimus, et domina : 155
[Et qui principio nobis te tradidit, a quo
  Sunt primo nobis omnia nata bona ;]
Et longe ante omnes, mihi quæ me carior ipso
    est,
  Lux mea ; quâ vivâ vivere dulce mihi est. 160

CARMEN XLVI.

De Inconstantiâ feminei Amoris.

Nulli se dicit mulier mea nubere malle,
  Quam mihi ; non si se Jupiter ipse petat.
Dicit : sed, mulier cupido quod dicit amanti,
  In vento et rapidâ scribere oportet aquâ.

CARMEN XLVII.

Ad Lesbiam.

Dicebas quondam, solum te nôsse Catullum,
  Lesbia : nec, præ me, velle tenere Jovem.
Dilexi tum te, non tantum ut volgus amicam,
  Sed pater ut natos diligit et generos.
Nunc te cognovi. Quare, etsi impensius uror,   5
  Multo mi tamen es vilior et levior.
Qui potis est? inquis. Quod amantem injuria
    talis
  Cogit amare magis, sed bene velle minus.

CARMEN XLVIII.

In Ingratum.

Desine de quoquam quidquam bene velle mereri,
  Aut aliquem fieri posse putare pium.
Omnia sunt ingrata : nihil fecisse benigne est :
  Immo etiam tædet, tædet obestque magis ;
Ut mihi, quem nemo gravius nec acerbius ur-
    get,   5
  Quem modo qui me unum atque unicum
    amicum habuit.

CARMEN XLIX.

Ad Lesbiam.

Nulla potest mulier tantum se dicere amatam
　　Vere, quantum a me, Lesbia, amata, mea, es.
Nulla fides ullo fuit unquam fœdere tanta,
　　Quanta in amore tuo ex parte reperta meâ est.
Nunc est mens adducta tuâ, mea Lesbia, cul-
　　pâ,　　　　　　　　　　　　　　　　　　　　5
　　Atque ita se officio perdidit ipsa pio,
Ut jam neç bene velle queam tibi, si optima fias,
　　Nec desistere amare, omnia si facias.

CARMEN L.

Ad se ipsum.

Siqua recordanti benefacta priora voluptas
　　Est homini, cum se cogitat esse pium,
Nec sanctam violâsse fidem, nec fœdere in ullo
　　Divûm ad fallendos numine abusum homines;
Multa parata manent in longâ ætate, Catulle,　5
　　Ex hoc ingrato gaudia amore tibi.
Nam, quæcùmque homines bene quoiquam aut
　　dicere possunt,
　　　7 *

Aut facere, hæc a te dictaque factaque sunt;
Omnia quæ ingratæ perierunt credita menti.

    Quare jam te cur amplius excrucies?   10
Quin te animo obfirmas, teque istinc usque re-
    ducis,
    Et, Dîs invitis, desinis esse miser?
Difficile est longum subito deponere amorem:
    Difficile est: verum hoc quâlubet efficias,
Una salus hæc est: hoc est tibi pervincendum. 15
    Hoc facies, sive id non pote, sive pote.
O Dî, si vostrum est misereri, aut siquibus un-
    quam
    Extremâ jam ipsâ in morte tulistis opem;
Me miserum adspicite; et, si vitam puriter egi,
    Eripite hanc pestem perniciemque mihi,   20
Quæ mihi subrepens imos, ut torpor, in artus,
    Expulit ex omni pectore lætitias,
Non jam illud quæro, contra ut me diligat illa,
    Aut, quod non potis est, esse pudica velit:
Ipse valere opto, et tetrum hunc deponere mor-
    bum.   25
    O Dî, reddite mî hoc pro pietate meâ.

CARMEN LI.

Ad Rufum.

Rufe, mihi frustra ac nequidquam credite amice ;
  Frustra ? immo magno cum pretio atque malo ;
Siccine. subrepsti mî, atque, intestina perurens,
  Mî misero eripuisti omnia nostra bona ?
Eripuisti. Heu ! heu nostræ crudele venenum 5
  Vitæ ! heu ! heu nostræ pestis amicitiæ !

CARMEN LII.

In Lesbium.

Lesbius est pulcher : quidni ? quem Lesbia
  malit,
  Quam te cum totâ gente, Catulle, tuâ.
Sed tamen hic pulcher vendat cum gente Catul·
  lum,
  Si tria notorum suavia reppererit.

CARMEN LIII.

Ad Juventium.

Nemone in tanto potuit populo esse, Juventi,
  Bellus homo, quem tu diligere inciperes,

Præterquam iste tuus moribundâ a sede Pisa ari
    Hospes, inauratâ pallidior statuâ?
Qui tibi nunc cordi est; quem tu præponere
    nobis   5
Audes.   Ah! nescis, quod facinus facias

CARMEN LIV.

Ad Quintium.

Quinti, si tibi vis oculos debere Catullum,
    Aut aliud, siquid carius est oculis;
Eripere ei noli, multo quod carius illi
    Est oculis, siquid carius est oculis.

CARMEN LV.

De Arrio.

Chommoda dicebat, si quando commoda vellet
    Dicere, et hinsidias·Arrius insidias;
Et tum mirifice sperabat se esse locutum,
    Cum, quantum poterat, dixerat hinsidias.
Credo, sic mater, sic Liber avunculus ejus,   5
    Sic maternus avus dixerit, atque avia.
Hoc misso in Syriam, requiêrant omnibus aures;

Audibant eadem hæc leniter et leviter;
Nec sibi postilla metuebant talia verba,
  Cum subito affertur nuntius horribilis,   10
Iōnios fluctus, postquam illuc Arrius îsset,
  Jam non Iōnios esse, sed *Hionios.*.

CARMEN LVI.

De Amore suo.

Odi et amo.   Quare id faciam, fortasse requiris.
. Nescio : sed fieri sentio, et excrucior.

CARMEN LVII.

De Quintiâ et Lesbiâ.

Quintia formosa est multis : mihi candida, longa,
  Rectâ est.   Hoc ego: sic singula confiteor.
Totum illud, formosa, nego : nam nulla venustas,
  Nulla in tam magno est corpore mica salis.
Lesbia formosa est ; quæ cum pulcherrima tota
    est,   5
  Tum omnibus una omnes surripuit Veneres.

CARMEN LVIII.

De Lesbiâ.

Lesbia mî dicit semper male, nec tacet unquam
  De me : Lesbia me, dispeream, nisi amat.
Quo signo ? quasi non totidem mox deprecor illi
  Assidue : verum dispeream, nisi amo.

CARMEN LIX.

In Cæsarem.

Nil nimium studeo, Cæsar, tibi velle placere,
  Nec scire, utrum sis albus an ater homo.

CARMEN LX.

De Smyrnâ Cinnæ Poëtæ.

" Smyrna " mei Cinnæ nonam post denique
    messem,
  Quam cœpta est, nonamque edita post hiemem ;
Millia cum interea quingenta Hortensius uno

      *   *   *   *   *

Smyrna cavas Atacis penitus mittetur. ad un-
    das;   5
    Smyrnam incana diu sæcula pervolüent.
At Volusî annales [Paduam morientur ad ipsam,]
    Et laxas scombris sæpe dabunt tunicas.
Parva mei mihi sunt cordi monimenta [laboris ;]
    At populus tumido gaudeat Antimacho.   10

CARMEN LXI.

Ad Calvum, de Quintiliâ.

Si quidquam mutis gratum acceptumque sepulcris
    Accidere a nostro, Calve, dolore potest,
Quo desiderio veteres renovamus amores,
    Atque olim amissas flemus amicitias;
Certe non tanto mors immatura dolori est   5
    Quintiliæ, quantum gaudet amore tuo.

CARMEN LXII.

Inferiæ ad Fratris Tumulum.

Multas per gentes et multa per æquora vectus,
    Adveni has miseras, frater, ad inferias,

Ut te postremo donarem munere mortis,
 Et mutum nequidquam alloquerer cinerem ;
Quandoquidem fortuna mihi tete abstulit ipsum, 5
 Heu, miser indigne frater ademte mihi !
Nunc tamen interea prisco quæ more parentûm
 Tradita sunt tristes munera ad inferias,
Accipe, fraterno multum manantia fletu :
 Atque in perpetuum, frater, ave, atque vale. 10

CARMEN LXIII.

Ad Cornelium.

Si quidquam tacito commissum est fido ab amico,
 Quojus sit penitus nota fides animi ;
Me unum esse invenies illorum jure sacratum,
 Corneli, et factum me esse puta Harpocratem.

CARMEN LXIV.

Ad Lesbiam.

Si quidquam cupidoque optantique obtigit un-
  quam, et
 Insperanti, hoc est gratum animo proprie :
Quare hoc est gratum, nobis quoque carius auro,
 Quod te restituis, Lesbia, mî cupido.

Restituis cupido, atque insperanti ipsa refers te 5
  Nobis.   O lucem candidiore notâ !
Quis me uno vivit felîcior ? aut magis hac quid
  Optandum vitâ dicere quis poterit ?

CARMEN LXV.

In Cominium.

Si, Comini, populi arbitrio tua cana senectus
  Spurcata impuris moribus intereat ;
Non equidem dubito, quin primum inimica bo-
    norum
  Lingua exsecta avido sit data volturio ;
Effossos oculos voret atro gutture corvus,   5
  Intestina canes, cætera membra lupi.

CARMEN LXVI.

Ad Lèsbiam.

Jucundum, mea vita, mihi proponis amorem
  Hunc nostrum inter nos, perpetuumque fore.
Dî magni, facite, ut vere promittere possit ;
  Atque id sincere dicat, et ex animo ;
8

Ut liceat nobis totâ producere vitâ 5
  Æternum hoc sanctæ fœdus amicitiæ.

CARMEN LXVII.

Ad Gellium.

Sæpe tibi studioso animo venanda requirens
  Carmina uti possem mittere Battiadæ,
Quîs te lenirem nobis, neu conarere
  Infestum telis icere, musca, caput;
Hunc video mihi nunc frustra sumtum esse la-
    borem, 5
  Gelli, nec nostras hinc valuisse preces.
Contra, nos tela ista tua evitamus amictu :
  At, fixus nostris, tu dabi' supplicium.

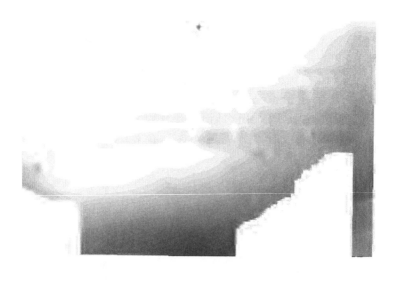

NOTES.

CARMEN I.

To Cornelius Nepos.

CATULLUS in these verses dedicates his volume of poems to Corn. Nepos, on account of the interest he had shown, in what Catullus modestly calls "his trifles," and the commendations he had bestowed upon them, in the midst of his own learned and laborious occupations.

1. *Quoi*] i. q. *cui.*

6. *Omne . . . chartis*] a general history in three volumes.

9. *patrona Virgo*] 'Minerva,' the patroness of wits. Voss reads *patroa*, meaning Vesta, to whom the first fruits were offered. Vide Ovid Fasti, 6, 304.

CARMEN II.

To the Sparrow of Lesbia.

Catullus mentions the various endearments and

sports with her favorite bird, with which Lesbia was wont to amuse herself, and soothe the ardor of her passion; and the delight with which he could indulge the same playful fondness. The lady whom he so often addresses under the name of Lesbia, was named Clodia, the sister, it is supposed, of the infamous Clodius.

7, 8.] In these verses I have followed the reading of Voss, who gives this explanation; "*credo te ó passer, nescio quid carum jocari cum meo desiderio nitenti i. e. cum puella mea, et similiter credo te solatiolum esse sui doloris, ut gravis ejus ardor acquiescat.*" Sillig reads,

Et solatiolum sui doloris
Credo, *ut, quum* gravis acquiescet ardor
Tecum ludere sicut ipsa *possem, &c.*

making *solatiolum* and *carum quid* accusatives dependent on *jocari,* and introducing the apodosis of the sentence with *ut quum; ut* for *utinam.*

11. *puellæ*] Atalanta, vide Ovid Met. Lib. 10.

CARMEN III.

A lament on the death of the Sparrow.

2. *quantum .. hominum*] conf. Carmen ii. v. 7.
10. *pipilabat*] i. q. *pipiabat.*

CARMEN IV.

The Dedication of the Barque.

The barque of Catullus which had borne him safely through the stormy and perilous seas from Pontus, and was now gratefully consecrated to the sailor's gods, recounts its own history and its own praises. The poet points out (*quem videtis*) the offering to his friends, as they pass by the Temple where it is hung.

1. *Phaselus*] Græce Φάσηλος a bean, a long, slender kind of vessel, distinguished by the form of its prow, which was long and extended obliquely over the water, now and for a long time in common use in the Mediterranean.

3, 4. *Neque ... Nequisse*] Two negatives, 'to have been able.'

13. *Amastri*] 'Amastris,' now Famastro, a city of Paphlagonia. *Cytore*] Virgil, 2d Georgic, 437.

18. *impotentia*] without self-control, i. e. 'raging.' So Carmen 25, v. 12. *impotente amore.*

22. *litoralibus Diis*] No particular class of deities is designated by the epithet *litorales.* Temples were erected on many shores, and promontories dedicated to various divinities, towards which the mariner offered his prayer, and where he paid his vows. *Neque ulla vota*] Because of the entire security the sailors felt in the excellence of their vessel. Vows were made only in the apprehension of extreme danger.

8 *

24. *Novissimo*] 'farthest,' in compliance with a notion of the early Greeks, who supposed Colchis to be the eastern limit of the world. Vide Ovid Trist. 3, 13, 27 ; so Carm. 38, v. 4. *casu novissimo,* 'the last (farthest) extremity of distress ;' *novissimum agmen,* 'the rear.' Livy, Lib. 21, 35. *lacum*] The Benacus, near which was Sirmio, the residence of Catullus. Vide notes to Carm. 23.

CARMEN V.

To Lesbia.

A graceful expression of a genuine Anacreontic sentiment, persuading her to indulge the delights of mutual affection, by urging the shortness of life, and the everlasting sleep which follows.

11. *ne sciamus*] That we may begin a new series.

13. *cum sciat*] He fears the fascination of some looker on. But no witness could harm them, unless he knew the name or the number of the thing to become the subject of his enchantments.

CARMEN VI.

To Lesbia.

A reply to Lesbia's question, how many kisses would satisfy his love.

4. *Laserpiciferis*] 'producing' benzoin, a plant much used for medicinal purposes. The best was produced in Cyrenaica. Pliny, Nat. Hist. xix. 15.

5. *æstuosi*] from the great heat of the surrounding region ; or perhaps from a spring there of a peculiar and changeable temperature.—Arrian Exped. Alex. Lib. 3, Sec. 4.

6. *Batti*] The first of that name, who emigrated from Theræ, and founded the royal family of the Battiadæ. Herodotus, Lib. 4, Sec. 150—159.

9. *basia basiare*] The verb beside its direct object takes the accusative of a word of the same meaning. This construction is more common among the Greeks, whom Catullus affects.

CARMEN VII.

To Verannius, on his return from Spain. Compare Horace, Carm. Lib. 1, 36.

2. *mihi*] *dativus commodi*, ' in worth to me,' ' in my estimation.'

CARMEN VIII.

The Mistress of Varrus.

Varrus, a friend of Catullus, finding him one day sauntering in the forum, invited him to visit his mistress. Among various topics of conversation, they spoke of Bithynia, where Catullus had recently served under Memmius. The natural inquiry being started, how far he had enriched himself there, he answered evasively, blaming the avarice of the prætors who governed the province; yet unwilling to appear to the lady entirely unsuccessful, he tells her that he had brought home half a dozen litter bearers. The wanton desires to borrow them, when the poet is compelled to get off with a lame and confused apology.

1. *Varri*] Vulpius, Turnebus and some others read *Varus*, and suppose the person here mentioned, to be Alphenus Varus, one of the most subtle and distinguished lawyers of his times—the same to whom Carm. xxii. was addressed. Vide Horace Sat. 3. Lib. 3. v. 130.

2. *ad s. a. visum*] the same as *visum suos amores.* Thus Terence Hecyra, Act 1. Scene 2. v. 189, has a similar construction, "*nostra (domina) it visere ad eam.*" So Plautus Bacch. Act 3. Sc. 5. "*Ibo et visam huc ad eum.*"

4. *Non illepidum*] 'not ungenteel.'

10. *prætoribus*] The same province was sometimes occupied by more than one prætor at once; or the reference may be to successive prætors.

12. *irrumator*] 'avaricious.'

13. *nec faceret pili*] 'valued not a hair.' Conf. Carm. xii. v. 17.

14. *illic natum*] 'what is said to have originated there.' Cicero in Verrem, says "*Nam ut mos fuit Bithyniae regibus lectica octophoro ferebatur.*

Verses 21, 22 and 23, are to be understood as a parenthesis, introduced to inform those to whom he is relating the adventure. *"Conversus ad lectores."* Vulp.

22. *grabati*] 'a small bed carried from place to place.' From the Greek κρασσατον, derived according to Voss, from επι το κρατα βαινειν, quasi καραβατον.

26. *ad Serapin*] The temple of Serapis was without the city, and was frequented for licentious purposes, and also for obtaining dreams there, which it was thought would aid in the recovery of health.

27—30.] These verses contain a strongly marked anacoluthon, the hesitating and broken confession of one detected in falsehood. The passage may be thus constructed, *Caius Cinna est meus sodalis ; is sibi paravit istud quod modo dixeram me habere, fugit me ratio. f. m. r.* 'I forgot myself.'

34. *negligentem*] scil. of his words.

CARMEN IX.

To Asinius.

Catullus sends this poem to Marrucinus Asinius, who in the freedom and carelessness of "mirth and wine," had secreted some foreign napkins, which he valued highly as memorials. of absent friends ; and threatens a poet's vengeance.

3.] Thefts of this kind were not infrequent. Conf. Carm. xix. v. 6. Martial Ep. 59. Lib. 8.

12. *æstimatione*] 'value.'

14. *Setaba*] Setabis was a town of Spain, on the river Sucro, famous for its very fine linen.

CARMEN X.

To Fabullus.

Our poet in his poverty does not forget, or the less relish the delights of social and festive enjoyment, and alleging the leanness of his larder, invites Fabullus to bring with him the means and accompaniments of his own supper; offering only his own affection, or if they should be preferred, odors which the goddess of Love had bestowed on his mistress.

CARMEN XI.

To Licinius Calvus.

A jocose rebuke to his friend Licinius, who on the Saturnalia, had sent him a vile poem, which he had received from one of his clients.

2. *munere isto*] 'for that present.'

3. *odio Vatiniano*] 'with the hatred of Vatinius.' Calvus had incurred the bitter enmity of Vatinius, by urging with great eloquence an accusation against him, of bribery. But see Lempriere's Class. Dict.

8. *repertum*] 'far-fetched,' or with Docring, "composed with much labor, in a new style."

9. *Sulla*] The individual here mentioned is supposed to have been a pedantic grammarian, the freedman of ·Sylla, who, as was often the case, took the name of his master.

11. *labores*] professional 'labors' in behalf of Sulla.

17. *si illuxerit*] 'when day shall have dawned.'

18. *Cæsios, Aquinios*] sorry poets.

19. *Suffenum*] a conceited verse maker. Conf. Carm. xvi.

CARMEN XII.

Catullus seems to have taken a violent dislike to a fellow townsman, whose jealousy was not so easily excited as his own, and whose complacent or heedless allowance of the sports and caprices of his wife, was intolerable to the hasty temper of the poet. He addresses the colony, offering his good wishes in the matter of a new bridge, which the residents very much desired, and asking in return, that the fellow who could so neglect his own interests, might be flung from it into the deepest and blackest mud beneath.

1. *Colonia*] Scaliger and Voss suppose that the place here mentioned was Novum Comum, a colony recently planted by Julius Cæsar. *ludere*] Certain contests, as boxing, were sometimes exhibited on bridges.

3. *asculis*] i. q. *assiculis*, 'slender beams.'

6.] 'On which (so good that) their sacred rites may be performed by the morris dancers.'

10. *ut*] i. q. *ubi*.

14. *cum*] i. q. *etsi*. *flore*] the greenness of her youth, as liable to errors; and also contrasted with the advanced age of her husband.

17. *uni*] for *unius*, as sometimes *toti* for *totius*, *alii modi* for *alius modi*.

18. *alnus . . . suppernata*] 'the alder hewn beneath,' i. e. a boat. *suppernata* is commonly written *subpernata*.

19. *Liguri*] 'of a Ligurian.' Liguria was noted for ship and boat timber.

20. *Tantumdem*] 'Just as much.'

22. *Nunc*] Sillig reads *hunc*. "*Hic is est, quem nolo.*" Better, for the notion of time is impertinent here, and *nunc* is never used, I believe, to denote sequence. *Hunc eum* is analagous to the common *hic ille*.

CARMEN XIII.

The dedication of a grove to Priapus, composed, probably during the poet's residence in Bithynia.

1. *dedico*] 'I devote.' *consecroque*] "I dedicate with solemn rites." "*Consecrare* has a more religious cast than *dedicare*." Dumesnil.

2. *Lampsaci*] Priapus was born at Lampsacus.

4. *ostreosior*] So Virgil George, 1. v. 207, *ostriferi fauces Abydi.*

CARMEN XIV.

An image of Priapus standing in a garden, addresses some mischievous boys, who were disposed to plunder on the grounds, mentions the various gifts and observances, by which the owner had sought to secure his favor, with his own duty of watchfulness, and points out to their rapacity, a richer vineyard and a more negligent Priapus.

This poem and the next, may be considered a *locus classicus* on the worship of Priapus. There are few passages, if any, in the whole of Latin literature, which more fully and strikingly evince, what we find it very difficult to comprehend, the earnest sincerity of the rustic worshipper. One can hardly rise from this truly poetical picture of the poor husbandman and his son in their devout offerings, without feeling that though the philosopher might despise, and the cultivated poet sneer or ridicule, yet they were influenced by a real faith in the power, and a real hope of the favor of the Deity they served.

4. *Nutrivi*] i. q. *auxi.* *ut*] with the force of *utpote*, 'because,' introducing the reason of the preceding sentence. *beata*] belongs to *quercus*, i. e.

9

Priapus. *"Auti illam villam quia quotidie muneri-*
bus et honoribus large afficior." Nam hujus villæ etc.
Sillig.

10. *ponitur*] 'is offered.'

15. *sed tacebitis*] Why silent? The common
answer, that the fruits of the earth only were pre-
sented to Priapus, is hardly satisfactory, as probably
in the time of Catullus, certainly soon after, sacrifices of blood were made to him. More likely, because they were offered only in the fouler mysteries,
which the darkness of midnight concealed from the
moral and severe, and which, therefore, he would
not have disclosed.

CARMEN XVI.

A satire upon Suffenus, a man of some preten-
sions to gentility, but a vile, voluminous and conceited poet. The piece naturally concludes with a
reflection on the blindness of men to their own
failings, and their tendency to mistake their own
powers.

1. *probe nôsti*] simply 'well known.'

5. *palimpsesto*] a material used for the first
draught of a work, from which it might be easily
erased.

6. *relata*] 'written out.' Carey suggests the
meaning "scored, blotted with corrections."

7. *umbilici*] The *umbilicus* was of two kinds: in cylindrical volumes, the inner edge of the roll, which was usually attached to a slender rod ; and in books made of two tables or pages, as those used for memoranda, a small button in the middle of each, to prevent their touching when closed, and obliterating the impression on the wax.

lora] The Romans attached to the outer edge of the volume, a strip of parchment, wide enough to fold around and enclose the whole. They were used for protection, and for ornament, and painted of various colors, here red.

8. *directa*] 'ruled.'

11. *abhorret*] scil. *a se ipso*. *mutat*] is often used passively.

12. *scurra*] 'a witling.'

14. *inficeto*] commonly written *infaceto*.

15. *Simul*] more frequently in prose we find *simul ac*. Horace uses *Simul*, Carm. Lib. 1. 12. v. 27. Catullus also, Carm. 35. v. 6. and 42. vs. 31. 12. 86. 147.

21. *manticæ*]

> " *Peras imposuit Juppiter nobis duas,*
> *Propriis repletam vitiis post terga dedit.*"
>
> Phaedrus. 4. 9.

CARMEN XVII.

To Furius.

A piece of severe satire upon Furius, whom he
ironically congratulates on the conveniences of his
extreme poverty, and the stinginess of his parents.

CARMEN XVIII.

To the young Juventius.

Catullus represents to Juventius, the low estate
of one who sought to win his affection, as a sufficient dissuasive, whatever other merits he might
possess.

1. *Juventiorum*] 'of the Juventii,' a family of con-
siderable distinction at Rome.

4. *mihi*] in passages like this, has commonly been
treated as an expletive. It may be better to consider
it as expressing the remote object of the verb, and in-
dicating more strongly than *mallem* would do without
it, the personal interest of the writer. Conf. Carm.
7. v. 2. and see Buttman's larger Greek Grammar,
Sec. 133, note 4. Voss conjectures *Midæ*, and
makes the sense of the line, that 'he would prefer
that Juventius should bestow the wealth of Midas
on his wooer.'

9. *hæc*] 'his condition and my wishes.' *elevaque*] 'undervalue.'

CARMEN XIX.

To Thallus..

Catullus with great severity and even coarseness, scolds and threatens Thallus, who had carried off and exhibited as his own, some articles belonging to him. This piece presents him in no very amiable light, yielding to violent passion, and descending to abusive language, on, to say the least, an unsuitable occasion. Such methods of gratifying ill-will, or revenging an affront, were not very uncommon in this age of Rome, and English literature, even is not wholly without examples. Catullus in these verses, has exhausted all the power of diminutives to abuse and degrade his enemy.

2. *oricillâ*] i. q. *auricula*, dim. of *auris*.

4. *diva mulier*] 'a female skilled in omens.' *occinentes*] 'whose song is of evil omen.'

6. *catagraphosque*] according to Voss, parchment tablets, painted of various colors, great numbers of which were made in Bithynia. 'Profiles'?

CARMEN XX.

To Furius.

The best reading of the first line of this poem is

9 *

entirely uncertain. The editions are divided, with great weight of authority on either side, between *nostra* and *vestra;* and I am not aware that we have any means of deciding the question. *Vestra,* seems to suit better with the general character and condition of Catullus. · Yet we do not know the time when it was written, or whether he was then prosperous or poor. Nor do we know the individual to whom it is addressed. In other pieces he speaks of two, of the same name, one a friend, and the other an enemy. Nor yet do we know the villa of which he speaks, as he possessed more than one, (Carm. 29. and 23.,) neither of which can be the one to which he here refers. The general construction of the piece needs no remark.

CARMEN XXI. ·

To a youthful Cupbearer.

2. *amariores*] 'more bitter,' i. e. older.

3. *magistræ*] the mistress of the revel, who prescribed the rule (*legem*) of drinking. The Postumia, who here held the office of symposiarch, is not known, probably a fancy name.

· 4. *acinâ Ebriosâ*] 'than the swollen grape.' Seneca makes this distinction between *ebrius* and *ebriosus.* "*Potest qui ebrius est, nunc primum esse, qui ebriosus est, sæpe extra ebrietatem esse.*"

7. *Thyonianus*] a name of Bacchus.

CARMEN XXII.

To Alphenus.

A remonstrance with Alphenus, who had gained and betrayed the confidence and affection of Catullus. The sentiment of the poem is sorrow rather than anger. The poet touches on the unfaithfulness of his friend, the tendency of such breaches of confidence to produce mutual distrust among men, and reminds him of the anger of the gods who guard the rights of friendship, and punish their violation.

CARMEN XXIII.

To the peninsula Sirmio.

This poem was composed on the occasion of the poet's return, care-worn and dejected, from his wearisome and fruitless expedition to Bithynia, to his beautiful and fondly-loved retreat at Sirmio. The feeling of home-joy which he expresses, is simple and natural, and every heart sympathizes with it.

"Sirmio was a peninsular promontory, of about two miles circumference, projecting into the lake Benacus, now the Lago di Garda."

"Sirmione appears as an island, so low and so narrow is the bank that unites it to the main land.

The promontory spreads behind the town, and rises into a hill entirely covered with olives. Catullus undoubtedly inhabited this spot, and certainly he could not have chosen a more charming retreat. The soil is fertile, and its surface varied; sometimes shelving in a gentle declivity, at other times breaking in craggy magnificence, and thus furnishing every requisite for delightful walks and luxurious baths; while the views vary at every step, presenting rich coasts or barren mountains, sometimes confined to the cultivated scenes of the neighboring shore, and at other times bewildered and lost in the windings of the lake, or in the recesses of the Alps."—Eustace, Classical Tour.

3. *uterque Neptunus*] *Neptunus stagnorum*, and *Neptunus maris*.

13. *Lydiæ*] from the origin of the northern Italians who emigrated from Lydia.

CARMEN XXIV.

To Diana.

This ode, one of the few strictly lyric poems of Catullus, was composed to be sung by choirs of youths and maidens, at the celebration of the Ludi Seculares, A. U. 700. For the date, see the observations of Voss on this ode, and for the character and purpose of the secular games, the remarks of

Mitscherlich, introductory to the Carmen seculare of Horace. This hymn celebrates the august origin of the goddess, and her various characters, and offices of aid and benevolence to men, and concludes with an invocation of her continued favor to the Roman people.

CARMEN XXV.

An invitation to Cæcilius.

Intended both to convey a compliment to the poetical skill of Cæcilius and to express his own affection.

3, 4. *Novi Comi*] *Novum Comum,* a town on the shores of the lake Larius, now di Como.

14. *Dindymi dominam*] Cybele; the phrase here used means a poem in praise of Cybele, composed by Cæcilius, the reading of which had gained him the ardent attachment of a learned lady of Comum.

18. *magna Mater*] 'the Cybele.' *inchoata*] 'finished.'

CARMEN XXVI.

On the Annals of Volusius.

The mistress of Catullus, during a period of estrangement, had vowed to Venus and Cupid, if she

ances, he had recovered his health. The poem seems aimed at Sextius, and through him, at those individuals, not infrequent at Rome, who inflict upon their guests, long and tedious recitations.

1.] This country residence of Catullus was situated on the borders of the Sabine and Tiburtine territory, and hence the doubt to which it belonged. Horace raises the same question in respect to his own villa. Lib. 2, Sat. 1, v. 34.

11. *Antius*] probably C. Antius Restio, the author of a sumptuary law. *petitorem*] 'candidate.'

19. *recepso*] for *recepero*.

CARMEN XXX.

To himself on the coming of Spring.

In this poem, Catullus expresses his delight, on leaving the cold plains of Phrygia, and the stormy Nicæa, for the warmer climate and renowned cities of the south; and bids farewell to his comrades, whom various pursuits now called to separate.

4. *Phrygii*] 'of Bithynia,' where Catullus passed a year with Memmius. In the division of the country which obtained in the time of Catullus, Bithynia was a part of *Phrygia major*.

5. *Nicææque*] a large city of Bithynia, on the lake Ascanius. *æstuosæ*] Bithynia was the coldest part of Pontus, according to Aristotle, (Prob. Sec.

25,) and Nicæa of Bithynia, and in summer the heat was no less remarkably excessive.

6. *Asiæ*] This term includes Ionia, and parts of Lydia and of Æolis.

CARMEN XXXI.

To Porcius and Socration.

Catullus is indignant that Porcius and Socration had become, by the favor of Piso, richer and more popular than his friends Verannius and Fabullus.

1. *sinistræ*] vide Carm. 9. v. 1.

2. *Pisonis*] Cneius, afterwards the associate of Cataline.

3. *Veranniolo*] diminutive of Verannius, Carm. 9. v. 17.

4. *verpus*] 'circumcised,' a term of severe reproach derived from the Jews, who were held in extreme contempt.

6. *de die*] unseasonable, 'during the day;' or as Voss, *repente* 'at any time, receiving many and sudden invitations.'

7. *vocationes*] 'invitations.'

CARMEN XXXIV.

To Licinius.

Catullus had passed a leisure day in framing

10

festive and mirthful verses, over wine, with Licinius, and had been charmed with his wit and humor. On parting, the remembrance of their pleasant meeting and a desire to renew it, made his night sleepless. He rises from his restless couch, and writes this poem to Licinius.

CARMEN XXXV.

To Lesbia.

This is a translation by Catullus, of the ode of Sappho, so highly praised by Longinus. Subjoined is an English translation from the Greek by Ambrose Philips. See the Spectator, No. 229.

"Bless'd as the immortal gods is he,
The youth who fondly sits by thee,
And hears and sees thee all the while
Softly speak and sweetly smile.

'Twas this deprived my soul of rest,
And rais'd such tumults in my breast;
For while I gazed, in transport tossed,
My breath was gone, my voice was lost;

My bosom glowed; the subtle flame
Ran quick through all my vital frame;
O'er my dim eyes a darkness hung;
My ears with hollow murmurs rung.

In dewy damps my limbs were chill'd;
My blood with gentle honors thrill'd:
My feeble pulse forgot to play;
I fainted, sunk, and died away."

Verses 8 and 12—16, in the text, printed in italics, and included in brackets, are doubtless an interpolation.

CARMEN XXXVI.

Catullus in these verses vents his indignation at the unworthy elevation of Nonius and Vatinius to curule offices.

CARMEN XXXVII.

To Camerius.

The poet writes to Camerius the pains he had taken, and the difficulties he had met, in trying to find him; and reproves the unkind secresy of his loves.

2. *tenebræ*] 'Lurking places.'

3. *minore Campo*] A smaller part of the Campus Martius, where the Roman youth practised their exercises; called *minor* in comparison with the portion in which the *comitia* were held.

6. *Magni*] 'the portico of Pompey.'

10. *pessimæ*] Conf. note on Carm. 26. v. 9.

22.] In the earlier editions, the following verses are arranged by themselves, as the conclusion of a poem left imperfect, with the title *Ad Camerium* The preceding verses seem to have in themselves such unity and completeness, as to make the supposition that they are an entire poem by themselves, very plausible. Yet they fit so well together from the general resemblance of subject, (which induced Scaliger and Doering to join them, and which may be done without impairing the requisite unity of the whole,) as to render it very probable that they were originally one.

23. *custos ille Cretum*] 'Talus,' a giant with a brazen body, fabled to have been given by Jupiter to Europa, and made guardian of the island of Crete ; which he went round three times every day. Plato, in his *Minos*, has given this explanation of the fable ; that Minos who made Rhadamanthus judge in the capital, committed the rest of the island to Talus, and that he thrice a year made a circuit through all the cities and villages of the country administering justice, according to laws which were engraved on tables of brass.

32. *quæritando*] Frequentative.

CARMEN XXXVIII.

A fragment of a poem of which we have neither the beginning nor the conclusion. Conf. Carm. 42. v. 154—7.

CARMEN XXXIX.

An Epithalamium on the Nuptials of Julia and Manlius.

The poem opens with an invocation to Hymen to aid the nuptial song, vs. 1—35, with various persuasives to induce his favoring presence, the grace and beauty of the bride, vs. 16—25, his power to enchain her affection, vs. 31—35. The poet then summons a choir of virgins to join his invocation, vs. 35—45, and returns to celebrate the praises of Hymen, in various virtues, and the love and veneration, and gratitude of men, vs. 46—75. He now turns to hail the approaching bride, and soothes her reluctant bashfulness, with praises of her beauty, and the honor and faithful love of her intended husband, vs. 76—110, alludes to various ceremonies and customary rites, the nuptial procession, the Fescemim verses, the scattering of nuts, the threshold that might not be touched, the separate banqueting of the bridegroom with his fellows; and having witnessed the entrance of the bride into her new house, after addressing the husband in a strain of high congratulation and compliment, he concludes in lines of exceeding beauty, with wishes for their highest bliss, and the consummation of their hopes and happiness, in a young Torquatus, who shall perpetuate his father's fame, and by his likeness attest his mother's virtues.

10 *

2. *Uraniæ genus*] Hymen, son of the muse Urania and Bacchus. Seneça Medea, v. 110.

With the sketch of Hymen in this and the following verses, compare Ovid, Heroides, 21. vs. 157—168.

18, 19. *Phrygiam Judicem*] Paris. A twofold resemblance is suggested, to the beauty of Venus and her success.

22. *Asia*] i. q. *Asiatica.* So Virgil Æn. 7. vs. 701–2, *Asia Palus*, a marshy tract on the banks of the Cayster. Homer, Il. β. 461.

24. *Ludicrum*] "*locus lusui aptum, lavacrum seu nympharium.*" Voss.

26. *aditum ferens*] v. 43. and Carm. 62. v. 79.

43. *bonæ Veneris*] 'Chaste Venus.'

44–5. *boni amoris*] 'honorable love.'

51. *tremulus*] 'trembling' with age, and therefore anxious to see his daughters married.

54. *timens*] 'in suspense,' fearing lest his hopes may be disappointed.

55. *captat aure*] 'catches with the ear,' i. e. listens attentively. Virgil Æn. 3. v. 514. *Palinurus auribus aera captat.*

61.] Claudian has a similar idea,

" *Nullum junxisse cubile*
Sine hoc, nec primas fas est attollere taedas."

Nupt. Pallad. et Celer. vs. 32–33.

65. *Comparier*] the ancient form of the infinitive.

68. *stirpe jungier*] Scaliger interprets this phrase not to be able to transmit an inheritance to ones children, which could not be done if they were illegitimate. For an heir when he enters upon an inheritance, perpetuates rather than succeeds to the rights of his father, who is thus said *stirpe jungier*.

72. *præsides*] 'Magistrates.' The poet means to express the dependence of well obeyed laws, and permanent magistracies on the sacredness of the marriage union.

76.] The bridal procession approaches.

87. *Aurunculeia*] 'Julia Aurunculeia.' Aurunculeius was a surname in the family of the Cottae.

96. *sis*] by syncope for *si vis*. Voss reads *st* 'hush,' and encloses *st* with *jam videtur*, in the parenthesis. '*Jam videtur*, and also *vidin? faces a. q. c.* may be an interrupting exclamation of some of the spectators, or rather of the poet addressed to the spectators.

114.] The hiatus in the manuscripts of the three preceding lines, by obscuring the connection and the sense, renders the reading of the clause in brackets, impossible to settle. The text is unquestionably corrupt.

127. *fescennina locutio*] Several specimen fescennine verses, may be found appended to

dian's poem, "*in Nuptiis Honorii et Mariae.*"
These, however, are mostly, no doubt, a departure
from the original idea of this species of composition.
The last only deserves the epithet *procax*, bestowed
by Catullus. For the origin of this kind of verses,
consult Horace Epist. Lib. 3. ep. 1. 145, and Dun-
lap's Roman Literature.

129. *desertum*] Scil. *se*, with which *amorem* in
the next line is in apposition.

131. *iners*] 'lazy,' an epithet of incitement.

133. *Lusisti nucibus*] 'indulged the follies and
levities of youth.' The allusion is to the services
he had yielded to the passions of his master.

134. *servire Thallassio*] The origin of this phrase
is given by Livy, Lib. 1. Sec. 9.

136. *villuli*] Your fellows have till now been vile
in your eyes, who have been admitted to the peculiar favors of your master. Some editions have
sordebam . . villice. Sillig *villicae.*

141. *male*] 'with difficulty.'

142. *glabris*] 'beardless boys,' whose intimacy he
had sought.

146–8.] The allusion in these and the preceding
verses to the licentious pleasures of Julius, in his
former life, in a manner which evidently implies
they were of course, and involved no dishonor, and
merited no reproach, occurring too, as it does in a
complimentary poem to a noble friend, from which

all that could offend would have been carefully ex-
cluded, presents one of the darkest shades in the
picture of Roman manners. Yet, while the passage
is essential to the entireness of the poem, it is also
of much value as an illustration of the moral sentiments of that age.

162. *anilitas*] means specifically the old age of
women, as *senectus* of men.

181. *mitte*] 'let go,' *dimitte*.

182. *prætextate*] Addressed to the youth who had
led the bride in the nuptial procession.

183. *adeant*] some editions read *adeat*.

186. *bonæ*] A common reading is *unis*, (*unis senibus bonae*) since the *pronubae* were usually selected
from the matrons who had been married only once.

206. *pulvis*] supposed to be contracted for *pulveris*. This however is believed to be the only
place in which *pulvis* is found in the genitive.
"*pulveris Africi.*" Sillig.

208. *subducat*] 'Enumerate.'

216. *Torquatus . parvulus*] Sir William Jones
has written an eloquent imitation of this passage,
(in an epithalamium on the marriage of Lord Spen-
cer,) which he declared worthy of the pencil of
Domenichino.

"And soon to be completely blest,
Soon may a young Torquatus rise,

Who, hanging on his mother's breast,
  To his known sire shall turn his eyes,
Outstretch his infant arms a while,
  Half ope his little lips and smile."

CARMEN XL.

This poem consists of alternate strains, sung by choirs of youths and maidens. After a brief contest on the merits and demerits of the evening star, whose rising marked the hour of their meeting, the maidens chant the praises of maidenhood, and the rival youths the worth and dignity of married life. The poem closes with an address to the lady, on whose nuptials it was composed, persuading her to lay aside her girlish bashfulness, and commit herself cheerfully and confidently to the arms of her husband. This is supposed to have been written on the same occasion with the preceding poem, having relation to a different portion of the ceremony, and in order of time preceding.

1. *consurgite*] A company of young men, the companions of the bridegroom, on the afternoon of his wedding day assembled at his house, at a banquet prepared for the occasion. At the first appearing of the evening star, they rose from the table and went out to meet the procession which attended the bride, and welcome her to her future home.

4. *Hymenæus*] 'nuptial song.'

6. *consurgite contra*] The group of maidens, mates of the bride, who accompanied her in the procession, seeing the young men approach, begin their song.

7. *Œtæos ignes*] From the summit of Œta the sun and stars were visible two hours earlier and later than from the vallies beneath. Heyne (ad Virg. Eclog. 8. v. 30.) supposes the general use of the epithet Œtæus by the poets, to have been derived from some Greek poet who lived in that vicinity, or wrote a poem on some event (as the nuptials of Peleus and Thetis) which occurred there. *Noctifer*] 'The harbinger of night.'

9. *canent*] 'intimate,' 'predict.' *quod visere par est*] '*visu digna.*'

11. *palma*] The parties were engaged in a contest of poetical and musical skill. The whole Carmen is a genuine specimen of the amœbean.

20.] Thus far preparation. The choir of girls now enter on their theme.

33. *Namque*] The reference indicated in *namque* is lost in the absence of the preceding line. Voss however, rejects the notion of a hiatus, and for *namque* reads *nempe*, giving the line an ironical sense.

34.] 'Thieves work undetected by night, whom after, you the same Hesperus returning with changed name, find the same. *quos eosdem*] 'the very same persons.' *mutato nomine*] as evening star, Hesperus; as morning star Phosporus.

[Several lines of heavily degraded text, largely illegible.]

36–7.] The youths reply with an insinuation that their competitors feel less indignation than they express.

The comparisons which follow, vs. 39—58, are hardly surpassed in elegance of expression and aptness of similitude, in any language.

45. *dum . dum*] *"prius dum significet quoad, sequens usque eo."*—Quint. Inst. Lib. 9. cap. 3.

CARMEN XLI.

Of Atys.

" Atys was a beautiful youth, probably of Greece, who, forsaking his home and parents, sailed with a few companions to Phrygia, and having landed, hurried to the grove consecrated to the great goddess Cybele. There struck with superstitious frenzy, he qualified himself for the service of that divinity; and snatching the musical instruments used in her worship, he exhorted his companions who had followed his example, to ascend to the temple of Cybele. At this part of the poem, we follow the new votary of the Phrygian goddess through all his wild traversing of woods and mountains, till at length, having reached the temple, Atys and his companions drop asleep, exhausted by fatigue and mental distraction. Being tranquillized in some measure by a night's repose, Atys becomes sensible of the misery of his situation, and struck with horror at his rash deed, he returns to the sea-shore. There he casts his eyes bathed in tears over the ocean homeward, and comparing his for-mer happiness with his present wretched condition, he pours forth a complaint unrivalled in energy and pathos. The violent bursts of passion are admira-bly aided by the irresistible torrent of words, and by the cadence of a measure powerfully denoting mental agony and remorse.* It is the only speci-men we have in Latin of the Galliambic measure, so called because sung by the Galli, the effeminate votaries of Cybele.

The story of Atys is one of the most mysterious of the mythological emblems. The fable was ex-plained by Porphyry; and the emperor Julian after-wards invented and published an allegory of this mystic tale. According to them, the voluntary emasculation of Atys was typical of the revolution of the sun between the tropics, or the separation of the human soul from vice and error." Dunlop.

Ovid (Fasti Lib. 4, vs. 223—244) gives a version of the story of Atys, quite different from that of Catullus.

The inscription of this poem is very various in

---

* Gibbon, however, in a spirit of juster criticism perhaps, speaks (History, chapter 33) "of the transition of Atys from the wildest enthusiasm to sober pathetic complaint for his irretrievable loss."

11

different editions. *De Attine* in Sillig, *Attis* in Voss, *de Attine furore percito* in others. Pansanias and Lucian write the name Αττης. Some manuscripts *Atthys.*

4. *vagus animi*] A Greek rather than a Latin construction, by which a word definitely limiting a general epithet, or proposition is put in the genitive. —See Matthiae Gr. Gram. sec. 339.

8. *citata*] mark the change of gender. *typanum*] i. q. *tympanum* in imitation of the τύπανον of the Greek poets, as well as for the sake of the metre. An instrument resembling very exactly our tamborine. v. 20. compare Carm. 42. v. 262.

9. *typanum*] in apposition with *tubam,* or used adjectively, the 'trumpet—*typanum.*' This instrument occupied the place of the *tubæ,* which were not used in the mysteries of Cybele. Cybelle] *metri causa.* Bentley ad Lucan. Phars. I. 600. writes Cybebe, and gives this rule, "*ut ubique scribendum est, quoties media syllaba protrahitur.*"

16. *truculenta pelagi*] *Truculenta* has the force of a substantive and governs the genitive, as is not uncommonly the case with neuter adjectives as well in the plural as in the singular.

18. *herae*] Atys.

21. *cymbalûm*] an instrument consisting of two circular plates of brass or steel, or concave with circular edges, which were held one in each hand,

and when struck together, produced a sharp ringing sound.

22. *Tibicen .. Phryx*] the Phrygian measure is celebrated for its exciting and maddening effects *vide* Quinct. Lib. I. cap. 10. *grave*] in opposition to acute.

43. *eum*] Referring to *somnus* v. 42. `Pasithea*] the wife of Somnus, quasi παςι θεὰ '*omnibus benigna*.'

71. *columinibus*] 'mountains.'

75. *nuntia*] 'tidings' neuter plural from *nuntium*.

78. *hinc*] Sillig has *hunc*, " *hunc* (sc, *Attinem*) *face ut redeat.*"

CARMEN XLII.

The Nuptials of Peleus and Thetis.

This is the longest and most highly wrought of the poems of Catullus, and may be ranked among the finest productions of the Latin Muse. It abounds in strikingly distinct descriptions, and pathetic and eloquent expressions of passion. The despairing anguish of the forsaken Ariadne, her reproaches mingled with love for her betrayer, are hardly any way inferior to the dying language of Dido, (Virg. Æneid 4.) and far superior to the strained sentiments and tamer expressions of the same Ariadne in Ovid. (Heroides, Ep. 10.) The picture of the sad daughter of Minos standing on the extreme beach—her hair loosened to the winds,

the veil which had hid her bosom, and her woven
girdle, fallen at her feet and tossed unheeded by
the waves, gazing after the vessel that bears away
her false lover, and forgetting all but the despair of
her own abandonment, is worthy of the highest
efforts of the sculptor or the painter. The con-
cluding verses (385 ad fin.) are in a tone of sad regret, and of severe morality, which the Poets of
Rome seldom attained.

The poem opens with a rapid sketch of the
Argonautic expedition, the surprise of the Pontic
sea nymphs, and the mutual attachment of Peleus
and Thetis. After a hasty congratulation, the Poet
passes to the scene of the nuptials, the thronging
of the Thessalian youth, who deserted the labors
of the field and of the vineyard—the palace and the
festal splendors of Peleus. Among the nuptial
ornaments is a curiously embroidered quilt, the
description of which and the narratives suggested
by it, comprise the longer part of the poem. On
one portion is represented Ariadne deserted by
Theseus on the shore of Naxos; in connection with
which the Poet relates the causes which led Theseus to Crete, the love and flight of Ariadne, and
the unhappy forgetfulness which proved the death
of Ægeus. On another part, is represented Bacchus enamored and pursuing Ariadne, and the
orgies of his attendants. Returning from this
episode, he introduces the Gods and Demi Gods

honoring the nuptials with their presence, and
bringing each his peculiar and appropriate gifts.
During the feast, the Parcae, whose persons and
labors are minutely described, sing a fit epithalamium, predicting the future glory of Achilles, the
promised offspring. The poem concludes in a
strain of touching mournfulness, contrasting with
the latter times, the blessedness of those days
when the celestials were wont to honor with their
presence the abodes and the solemn assemblies of
men; and dwells in a few sad lines on the crimes
which had withdrawn from men the friendship and
fellowship of the Gods.

5. *Colchis*] dative plural, 'the Colchians.'

8. *Diva*] Minerva. Hor. Lib. I. vol. 7. "*intactae
Palladis arces.*" *quibus*] referring to *juvenes* v. 4.

9. *Ipsa*] this labor is ascribed to Minerva, by
Seneca, Medea v. 365. and by Claudian de bello
Getico, v. 16.

11. *Illa*] sc. *carina. imbuit*] "*imbuere est proprie inchoare et initiare.*" Servius. *Amphitriten*] 'the
sea,' here the Pontic sea, for Catullus afterwards
mentions the voyage of Theseus as anterior.

14, 15.] are thus construed by Voss, *emersere
aequoreae Nereides e candenti gurgite admirantes
monstrum feri vultus. monstrum feri vultus—the
Argo*. To construe *Nereides* in apposition with *feri
vultus* may seem better to accord with the simple and
natural arrangement usually preferred by Catullus.

11 *

21. *sensit*] Voss reads *sanxit*, from the conjecture of Pontanus. If this were preferred, pater *ipse* would of course refer to Jupiter.

27. *suos . . . concessit amores*] Jupiter had loved Thetis, but was induced to resign her, as the fates had ordained according to the prediction of Prometheus, that the offspring of Thetis should become greater than his father. Quinct. Lib. 3. cap. 7.

28. *Neptunine*] patronimic.

29, 30.] Oceanus and Tethys begot Nereus and Doris, and they the Nereids, of whom Thetis.

35. *Scyros*] a distant island, but once subject to the Thessalians. *Phthiotica Tempe*] Tempe in Phhiotis. The word Tempe first used to designate a small and delightful portion of the valley of the Peneus, was afterward applied to any spot distinguished for its pleasantness.

36. *Cranonis . . Larrissea*] both towns of Thessaly.

43. *Ipsius*] 'of Peleus.'

49. *purpura*] equivalent to *hæc vestis*, v. 50. Hor. Lib. 2. Od. 18. v. 8.

52. *Diæ*] commonly supposed to be Naxos. Some however say the small island lying just off the shore of Crete, a little north-west of Panormus. See Plutarch Vita Thes.

60. *Minois*] 'daughter of Minos.'

61. *bacchantis Evæ*] "*mulieris Bacchi furore correptae et Evoe Evoe clamantis.*" Vulpius. See v. 256.

75. *injusti regis*] from the cruel war he waged and the tribute he imposed on Athens. This Minos was a grandson of the Cretan Minos so famed for the equity of his laws.

83. *funera .. ne funera*] 'mourned as dead while living.' Isocrates speaking of the same event, uses the expression πενθουμένους ἔτι ζῶντας. Encomium Helenae sec. 13.

96. *Golgos*] a place in Cyprus, sacred to Venus.

103. *frustra*] in relation to the desired affection of Theseus.

104. *tacito labello*] 'with whispered prayer.' The epithet *tacitus* is applied usually where the object of the prayer is impious or improper. Persius Sat. 2, v. 5. "*tacita libavit acerra.*" compare Horace, Lib. 1. Ep. 16, v. 60. "*labra movet metuens audiri,*" and in the fourth book of Tibullus, Carm. 5, v. 18. Here the prayer of Ariadne for the safety of Theseus might imply that she ceased to mourn for the loss of her brother.

145. *apisci*] for *adipisci*.

150. *germanum*] the Minotaur.

159. *parentis*] Ægeus the father of Theseus, as is evident from the succeeding lines. *prisci*] 'old' hence severe to the fancies of his son.

179. *invidit*] 'denies.'

179. *æquor*] from *æquus*, properly means 'the surface.'

180. *quemne*] observe the negative force of *ne* in this line, as also in v. 183.

217. *Reddite*] vocative participle. Theseus was born in the extreme old age of Ægeus.—Plutarch Vita Thesei.

227. *Itoni*] a town of Thessaly, from which the Athenians are said to have derived the worship of Minerva.

232. *Ætas*] 'time.' so v. 238, commonly a limited period.

236.] unquestionably a spurious verse.

239. *mandata*] subject of *liquére* understood.

252. *parte ex alia*] sc. *vestis.*

299.] The only nuptials of mortals which were honored by the presence of the Gods.—Isocrates, Evagoras, 6.

301. *Idri*] a mountain of Caria, where were many spots sacred to Apollo and Diana.

308. *quercus*] *erat* is understood. Habited in branches of oak, or perhaps in robes inwoven with oak leaves. The oak was an oracular tree.

309. *Tyro*] the daughter of Salmoneus. *orâ*] 'border' Theocritus, Pharmac. vs. 121, 2, speaks of a wreath of poplar entwined with purple ribbons.

312—314.] 'The right hand, with the fingers turned upward, first draws the thread, then with the thumb reversed whirls the spindle.'

324.] addressed to Peleus.

325. *nato*] Achilles.

342.⟩ Homer everywhere calls him πόδας ὠκύς.

347. *tertius hæres*] Agamemnon. Pelops left his kingdom to Atreus his son, Atreus to Thyestes his brother, and Thyestes to Agamemnon his nephew, the son of Atreus.

382. *putrida*] 'wasted' by age. *variabunt*] 'discolor.'

402. *primævi*] 'yet in early manhood.'

403. *innuptæ .. novercæ*] 'a daughter-in-law widowed by the death of her husband.' Sallust, Bell. Cat. 15.

404.] an allusion perhaps to Œdipus.

CARMEN XLIII.

To Hortalus.

Catullus had promised Hortalus a translation or imitation of the poem of Callimachus, entitled *de Coma Berenices*, but had been long delayed in executing this promise, by his grief for the loss of a tenderly loved brother. He at length sends him the poem from Callimachus completed, with this poetical apology for his delay. In many manuscripts this is found as the introductory portion of the following poem.

2. *Hortale*] supposed to be Marcus Hortalus, or Ortalus the grandson of Hortensius.

14. *Daulias*] 'the Daulian,' Procne. For the story of Procne and Itys, see Ovid Metam. Lib.

6. v. 620, seq. In the Heroides, Ep. 15. v. 154, he calls her *Daulias ales.*

16. *expressa*] 'translated' or 'closely imitated.' *Battiadæ*] of Callimachus, a native of Cyrene, and deriving his name, probably, from his descent from the royal family of Battus.

CARMEN XLIV.

The hair of Berenice.

Berenice was the sister and wife of Ptolemy Evergetes, king of Egypt. A few days after his marriage, he was called away to a war in Syria, and Berenice, offering supplications for his safe return, vowed, should her prayers be answered, to consecrate her hair to the gods (*multis Deorum, v. 9.*) The offering immediately and mysteriously disappeared from the temple, and Conon, a celebrated mathematician and astronomer of Samos, soon discovered it changed into a constellation in the heavens; and Callimachus who resided at Alexandria, willing likewise to gain favor at court, wrote a poem on the event, which, except a few fragments, is now lost, and of which this of Catullus is a version. The constellation is introduced relating the causes which separated itself from the head of Berenice, and expressing regrets for its absence, which the brilliance of its new position could not suppress.

5. *Latmia*] a mountain of Caria, the dwelling of Endymion.

7. *cælesti lumine*] construe with *fulgentem.*

15. *Estne n. n. o. v.*] 'is Venus odious to young brides?' The transition here is abrupt. The order of thought seems to be this. Are the maidenly reluctance of young brides, and their timid apprehensions of their coming nuptials, real or feigned? The sorrow and vows of Berenice on the departure of her new married husband, teach me they are not sincere.

16. *frustrantur*] 'mocked.'

17. *fundunt*] sc. *novae nuptae.*

21. *luxti*] for *luxisti.*

26. *magnanimam*] Hyginus, (Poet. Astron. cap. 24.) mentions as instances of the masculine character of Berenice, and which secured to her the throne of Egypt, a passion for horses, and her habit of sending them to contend in the Olympic games. Also, that once when Ptolemy, her father, sought safety in flight from more numerous forces, she rallied the flying troops, and defeated the enemy.

28. *alis*] for *alius.*

30. *tristi*] for *trivisti.*

36. *Asiam*] i. e. Syria.

39. *invita*] So Virgil, Æn. 6. 460. *Invitus Regina tuo de litore cessi.* In these expressions of passionate regret, the original author addressed to the princess most courtly adulation. A similar strain

of compliment is . implied in the preceding verses, in the intimations that her love and fears, had overcome her wonted energy, and self-possession.

41. *quod*] sc. *caput. inaniter*] "*ut solent perjuri.*" *digna ferat*] let him suffer due punishment.

42. *postulet*] 'arrogate to himself,' 'boast.'

44. *Progenies Thiæ*] 'the Sun.'

51. *paulo ante*] join with *sorores*. 'just now sister locks.' *abjunctæ*] i. e. 'whom I have left behind.'

53. *unigena*] Zephyrus twin brother (Carm. 42. v. 201,) of Memnon; both born of Aurora.

54. *ales equus*] in apposition with *unigena*, v. 53. *Arsinoës Chloridos*] Arsinoë the mother adoptive of Berenice, was worshipped by the Egyptians, under the name of Chloris.

57. *Zephyritis*] the same as Arsinöe Chloris, v. 54, so called from a temple dedicated to her and Venus, on the Zephyrian promontory.

66. *Callisto*] dative case.

65–67.] these verses determine the position of the constellation, having Bootes on the east, Leo on the west, northward the fore feet of Ursa Major, southward Virgo.

69, 70.] in compliance with the popular belief, that the stars occupy the heavens only in the night, and on the return of day pass into the ocean. *vestigia*] 'footsteps.'

71. *pace tuâ*] lest this seeming boasting should excite the indignation of Nemesis.

77, 78.] Voss reads *expers* for *explens*, and *murrae* for *una*, asserting that virgins were not used to smear their hair with unguents, but used simply myrrh or oil. Sillig joining *omnibus expers* with *virgo*, reads,

> *Dum virgo quondam fuit omnibus expers,*
> *Unguentum multa millia bibi.*

79-82.] this passage seems to have perplexed commentators very much, and almost every one has given a different construction, Compare Vulpius, Voss, &c. The order is *vos, quas taeda optato lumine junxit non* (i. e. *ne*) *tradite corpora, nudantes rejecta veste papillas, unanimis conjugibus, prius quam onyx libet mihi jucunda munera.*

89. *tu*] Berenice.

90-93.] *effice me esse tuam,* (restored to thee,) *non votis, sed largis muneribus.*

94. *Hydrochöei*] (ὑδῶρ χεῶ) 'Aquarius,' dative case. *Oarion*] i. q. Orion. Both are constellations, whose appearing was usually accompanied with storm, and the sense may be "let me be restored, the tresses of a queen, though there should be perpetual storm." Or perhaps, 'let Aquarius and Orion retain their splendor in the heavens, let me,' &c.

12

CARMEN XLV.

To Manlius.

The poet begins this letter to Manlius, by rendering him thanks for the friendship which induced him in his affliction, to apply to himself for consolation; and mentions the loss of his brother, and the inconvenience of his situation at Verona, as an excuse for omitting to comply with his request. The remainder of the poem is occupied with the praises of Manlius, allusions to the kindness Catullus had received from him, and a somewhat long digression in praise of a lady, to whose favor he had been introduced by Manlius.

10. *Muneraque et Musarum .. et Veneris*] i. e. "*versiculos amatorios.*"

17. *lusi*] 'indulged in poetic essays.' Carm. 38. v. 2.

34. *capsula*] a box usually "cylindrical, in which manuscripts were placed vertically with the titles at the top."

73. *inceptam frustra*] 'entered in vain,' as she was so soon to be separated from her husband, *domum*, v. 72, has the sense of family 'home.'

77. *desideret ara cruorem*] the displeasure of the gods was incurred by the omission of some customary nuptial sacrifices.

83. *scibant*] 'ordained.'

107. *Quale*] the deep love of Laodamia is grossly compared to the abyss under mount Cylleve. Hercules, it is said, driven by Eurystheus from Tirinthia, went to Pheneus, a city of Arcadia, and as the Olbius by its overflow, had made the adjacent country an immense marsh, he drained off the waters by an excavation of fifty stadia in length, which passed under the neighboring mountains.— Pausanias, Archaica, cap. 14.

110. *audit*] 'is said;' for a similar use of *audit*, see Horace, Ep. 1. 14. 17, and Serm. 2. 7. 101. In a similar sense the Greeks sometimes use ἀκούειν, as Xenophon, Anab. Lib. vii. cap. 7. Sec. 23. εὖ ἀκούειν "to hear ones self (i. e. to be) well spoken of."

112. *heri*] Eurystheus.

113. *ut*] pointing to the destiny assigned to Hercules by the fates as the end and reward of his labors.

116. *indomitam*] sc. *se*, Laodamia.

117–122.] a comparison of her affection with the doting on the son of an only daughter, of a grandfather whose hopes of perpetuating his name had been given up, and whose property must have passed to hated and fortune-hunting relatives. *inventus*] as an heir. *vulturium*] 'the vulture,' i. e. the legacy-hunting relative.

123.] compare Carm. 2.

126.] he commends the constancy of Laodamia, in contrast with the fickleness of her sex. This verse is to be connected with v. 117, *Nam neque*, &c.

129, 130.] the whole episode of Laodamia, seems intended to set forth by comparison the worth of Catullus's mistress.

CARMEN XLVII.

To Lesbia, on the detection of her inconstancy.

1. *nôsse*] primarily, 'to know,' here in imitation of an occasional use of the Greek γινώςκω, it implies affectionate regard, 'to have been intimate with.'

3. *dilexi*] *diligere* properly means to esteem.

5. *cognovi*] *cognoscere*, means specifically to discover, as *agnoscere* to recognize.

7. *injuria talis*] by throwing obstacles in this way inflamed his passion, (*cogit amare magis*,) though it diminished his good will (*bene velle.*)

CARMEN XLVIII.

On an Ingrate.

2. *pium*] with its kindred *pietas* &c. seems to have the general signification of 'regardful of duty,' the particular duty or relation to be determined from the context; here 'grateful.'

3.] construe, *fecisse benigne est nihil.*

5. *ut mihi*] 'as to me,' 'in my case.'

CARMEN XLIX.

To Lesbia.

3. *fœdere*] an allusion to the constancy and lasting

obligation of the marriage relation which *fœdus* often signifies.

4. *amore tuo*] Catullus has not regarded the distinction which commonly obtains, between *amore tuo* and *amore tui.*

6. *pio*] 'constant.'

CARMEN L.

To himself.

Saddened by the unfaithfulness of Lesbia, and conscious of his own weakness, Catullus pleads his own fidelity, and earnestly and seriously prays to the gods to be delivered from the power of his love for her.

4. *Divûm . . numine abusum*] by perjury.

11. *usque*] 'forever.'

12. *Diis invitis*] "Venere et Amore invitis."

26. *pietate*] 'constancy.'

CARMEN LI.

To Rufus.

A false friend and a successful rival.

CARMEN LII.

On Lesbius.

A man of unkissable lips, but whom Lesbia preferred to Catullus.

12 *

4. *notorum*] 'of his acquaintance.'

CARMEN LIII.

To Juventius.

A young Roman, whom Catullus reproves and ridicules for having preferred to himself a jaundice visaged Pisaurian.

CARMEN LIV.

A neatly expressed epigram addressed to Quintius, probably a rival with Catullus in the favors of Aufilena.

CARMEN LV.

Of Arrius.

A Roman cockney, who made himself notorious by an affected pronunciation.

8. *eadem hæc*] 'these same' words, to which Arrius had given the aspirate. *leniter ac leviter*] 'softly and lightly.'

9. *postilla*] i. q. *postea*.

CARMEN LVII.

Of Quintia and Lesbia.

Catullus compares Quintia, who was esteemed a

great beauty, with his own Lesbia, allowing to Quintia many beauties, but denying her claim to be called beautiful.

3. *venustas*] 'grace.'
4. *salis*] 'elegance.'

CARMEN LVIII.

Of Lesbia.

Love surviving disdain and reproaches.

3. *deprecor*] seems here to have not merely the force of 'to pray against,' to deprecate, but also includes the notion of imprecation. So many maledictions as Lesbia utters against him, he forthwith and continually invokes on her.

CARMEN LIX.

On the Smyrna of the Poet Cinna.

Fragments of a poem in which Catullus gives his opinion of the worth of several cotemporary writers, and of their prospects of immortality.

1. *Smyrna*] the name of an elaborate poem of Cinna. This was an intimate friend of Cæsar and of Catullus, (*mei*) Corn. Helvius Cinna.
3. *Hortensius*] *Quintus* the celebrated orator.
6. *pervolvent*] 'turn over,' 'read.'

7. *Volusi annales*] vide Carm. 26.

8.] for the use of fishmongers in wrapping up fish.

10. *Antimacho*] a native of Colophon, who wrote a huge poem on the Theban war.

CARMEN LX.

To Licinius Calvus.

On the early death of Quintilia, solacing his grief with the hope that if an affectionate remembrance by the survivors, may be grateful to the departed, the sadness of her untimely loss of the joys of life, would be overpaid by the strength and constancy of his love.

CARMEN LXI.

Catullus had gone to Troas, to pay the last honors to the Manes of his brother, who was buried there. After the usual solemnities, he addresses the dead in the words of this poem. The love of Catullus for his brother, the only relative he mentions, is one of the brighter features in a character too deeply stained with the licentiousness of the age.

CARMEN LXII.

He commends to his friend Cornelius, his power of keeping secrets.

3. *illorum jure sacratum*] 'bound by the oath of such.'

4. *Harpocratem*] the god of Silence.

CARMEN LXIII.

To Lesbia.

On the unexpected renewal of her attachment to him.

CARMEN LXIV.

On Cominius.

Whose license of his tongue, and crimination of virtuous citizens, had made him universally odious.

CARMEN LXV.

To Lesbia.

From whom he had been estranged, on her offering a reconciliation ; expressing a prayer for its sincerity and permanence.

CARMEN LXVI.

To Gellius.

1. *studioso animo venanda*] 'to be studied with

thoughtful mind,' applied to a poem of Callimachus, obscure and full of invective against Apollonius Rhodius, of which Catullus had attempted an imitation, against Gellius. Ovid *in Ibide,* v. 55. *seq.,* in allusion to these,

> *carmina Battiadae,*
> *Nunc, quo Battiades inimicum devovet Ibin,*
> *Hoc ego devoveo teque tuosque modo.*
> *Utque ille, historiis involvam carmina caecis :*

4.] *Tela infesta meum mittere inusque caput.*

Sillig.

7. *contra*] still, 'but yet.'

SCHOOL AND CLASSICAL BOOKS,

PUBLISHED BY

PERKINS & MARVIN,

No. 114 *Washington Street, Boston.*

INTRODUCTION TO THE ECLECTIC
READER; A selection of Familiar Lessons, designed
for Common Schools. By B. B. EDWARDS.

THE ECLECTIC READER, designed for
Schools and Academies. By B. B. EDWARDS.

THE SCHOLAR'S COMPANION; or a
Guide to the Orthography, Pronunciation, and Deri-
vation of the English Language : containing, besides
several other important improvements, extensive tables
of words deduced from their Greek and Latin Roots.
Designed for Schools and Academies, and also for
students in Elocution. Arranged on the basis of the
Fifteenth London Edition of Butter's Etymological
Spelling Book and Expositor. By RICHARD W.
GREEN.

ELEMENTARY TREATISE ON THE
CONSTRUCTION AND USE OF MATHE-
MATICAL INSTRUMENTS, usually put into Por-
table Cases.

ELEMENTARY GEOMETRY, both Linear, Plane, and Solid. By N. J. LARKIN, teacher of Geometry, Author of the Rudiments of Geometry, and the Introduction to Solid Geometry.

THE GREEK PRIMITIVES of the Mes- sieurs De Port Royal. To which are added Rules for Derivation, or the Formation of Words. Selected principally from Buttman's Greek Grammar.

SELECT LETTERS OF PLINY THE YOUNGER, with Notes illustrative of the Manners, Customs, and Laws of the Ancient Romans. For the use of Schools.

CPSIA information can be obtained
at www.ICGtesting.com
Printed in the USA
LVHW021457020220
645565LV00017B/960